Education in India during British Period

JAGDISH CHAND
Former Deputy Director of Education and
Executive Diretor of the Delhi Bureau of Textbooks,
Delhi Administration

ANSHAH
Anshah Publishing House

(2009, First Published in India in 2007)

Rs. 700

ISBN: 978-81-8364-021-3

2020 Impression

Education in India during British Period

Published by:
ANSHAH PUBLISHING HOUSE
LG 18-19, Pankaj Central Market,
Patparganj, Delhi 110092, India
Ph.: +91 11 47322068, 9650028065
Email: info@shiprapublication.com
Website: www.shiprapublication.com

Preface

The book Development of Education System in Ind published in 2004, provides comprehensive description an analysis of the development of education system from Vedi times to modern times. As per the requirement of market and demand of curriculum prescribed in various universities, the book covering a particular period is brought out independently for the benefit of students and educators. It is hoped that this volume Education in India during British Period will be welcomed and its advantage also taken by the pre-service and in service teachers.

The volume derives its material from several original and secondary sources and the author is grateful to all the authors and their publishers.

Jagdish Chand

Contents

1

Macaulay's Minute (1835)

BRIEF LIFE SKETCH OF MACAULAY (1800-1859)

Thomas Babington Macaulay, who is generally regarded as the architect of the system of education in India during the British rule, was a great essayist, historian, linguist, orator, politician, statesman and thinker. He was regarded as one of the first rate literary figures of his times. As a Parliamentarian, he made his mark in British Parliament. He came to India in 1838 and joined as the Law Member of the Executive council of the Governor-General. He was also appointed as the President of the General Committee on Public Instruction by Governor General Lord William Bentinck.

ESSENCE OF MACAULAY'S MINUTE

Macaulay wrote his famous Minute on Feb. 2, 1835 in which he vehemently criticised almost everything Indian: astronomy, culture, history, philosophy, religion etc., and praised everything western. On this basis he advocated the national system of education for India which could best serve the interest of the British empire. His minutes was accepted and Lord William Bentinck issued his proclamation in March 1935 which set at rest all the controversies and led to the formulation of a policy which became the corner stone of all educational programmes during the British Period in India.

CIRCUMSTANCES LEADING TO MACAULAY'S MINUTE

(a) Revival of the Charter

The beginning of the State system of education in India under the British Rule may be traced back to the year 1813 when the East India Company was compelled by the force of circumstances to accept responsibility for the education of the Indians. Clause 43 of the Charter Act of 1813 which stated, "It shall be lawful for the Governor General-in-Council to direct that out of any surplus which may remain of the rents, revenues, and profits arising from the said territorial acquisitions, after defraying the expenses of the military, civil and commercial establishment and paying the interest of the debt, in manner hereinafter provided, a sum of not less than one lac of rupees in each year shall be set apart and applied to the revival and improvement of literature and the encouragement of the learned natives of India and for the introduction and promotion of a knowledge of the sciences among the inhabitants of the British territories in India."

The Charter Act of 1813 did not specify the methods to secure the objects of, 'revival and improvement of literature', 'the encouragement of learned natives of India' and 'the introduction and promotion of a knowledge of sciences among the inhabitants of the British territories in India'. The vagueness of Clause 43 of the Charter Act of 1813 intensified the Oriental Occidental Educational Controversy in India. Since the dawn of 19th century, there had emerged two groups among the officials of the Company. One group was of the Orientalists or Classicists who wanted the promotion of Indian education through the medium of Sanskrit, Arabic and Persian, where as the other group was of Anglicists or Occidentalists who were in favour of developing western education in India through the medium of English.

(b) Points of Controversy on the Interpretation of Charter Act of 1813 and the National System of Education and Macaulay's Role

At that time, a major Oriental (classical) and Occidental controversy between the Orientalists (classists) and the Anglicists (Occidentalists) was going on in respect of the following issues:

1. *Aim of Education of the British Policy*: Whether it should be to educate the classes in higher branches of learning or the masses in elementary education.
2. *Type of Knowledge*: Whether to preserve and promote oriental learning (learning of the East) or to introduce Western knowledge, culture and science.
3. *Medium of Instruction*: Whether English or Persian and Sanskrit in Bengal, English or Indian languages in Bombay and Madras should become the medium of instruction. It may be recalled that at that time the Presidencies/Provinces of Bengal, Bombay and Madras contained numerous areas which now form new states like Orissa, Bihar, Bengal, Tamil Nadu etc.
4. *Agency of Education*: Whether the Government should assume direct responsibility of educating the Indians or the indigenous system of the country to continue.
5. *Missionaries*: Whether the shores of India to be thrown open to missionaries of all parts of the world to promote education or to a few missionaries or not at all.

There were important English Officers of the East India Company who were the supporters of the oriental point of view. H.T. Princep, who was the Education Secretary in Bengal was the leader of the Orientalist Group. On the contrary some prominent Indians like Raja Rammohan Roy supported the Anglicists who were in favour of English and Western learning.

EXTRACTS FROM MACAULAY'S VIEWS WHICH BECAME THE CORNERSTONE OF THE SYSTEM OF EDUCATION IN INDIA

Macaulay in his Minute made the following observations.

(i) "A single shelf of a good European literature was worth the whole native literature of India and Arabia."

(ii) Regarding imparting instruction through the media of Arabic, Persian and Sanskrit, he wrote, "We are to teach false history, false astronomy, false medicine, because we find them in the company of false religion."

(iii) About the claim of English language, he stated, "It stands pre-eminent even among the languages of the West... It is likely to become language of commerce throughout the seas of the East."

(iv) Regarding the utilisation of money at the disposal of the Governor General-in-Council, he said, "I hold his Lordship to be quite free to direct that it shall no longer be employed in encouraging Arabic and Sanskrit."

(v) On the publication of Indian books he wrote, "We are a Board for wasting public money, for printing books which are of less than the value of the paper on which they are printed while it was blank."

(vi) About Indian culture philosophy and science, he made these damaging remarks, "Absurd physics, absurd metaphysics, absurd theology."

(vii) The concluding observations reflect very clearly his firm resolve to pursue his policy, "If the decision of his Lordship in Council should be such as I anticipate, I shall enter on the performance of my duties with the greatest zeal and alacrity. If, on the other hand, it be the opinion of Government that the present system ought to remain unchanged, I beg that I may be permitted to retire from the chair of the Committee." His views were accepted by the Governor General William Bentinck.

Main Aim of Introducing English System of Education in India

Macaulay wrote in his Minute, "We must at present do our best to form a class of persons, Indian in blood and colour, but English in taste, in opinions, in morals and in intellect."

Macaulay's Arguments in Favour of English: Macaulay rejected the claims of Arabic and Sanskrit as against English, because he considered that English was better than either of them. His arguments in favour of English were:

1. It is the key to modern knowledge and is, therefore, more useful than Arabic or Sanskrit.
2. It stands pre-eminent even among the language of the West. In India, English is the language sponsored by the ruling class. It is likely to become the language of commerce throughout the seas of the East.
3. It would bring about renaissance in India, just as Greek or Latin did in England or just as the languages of Western Europe in civilised Russia.
4. The natives are desirous of being taught English and are not eager to learn Sanskrit or Arabic, and that demand of the latter was maintained artificially through, "bounty money".
5. It is possible to make the natives of this country good English scholars, and to that end our efforts ought to be directed.
6. It was impossible to educate the body of people, but it was possible through English education to bring about "a class of persons, Indian in blood and colour, but English in tastes, in opinions, in morals and in intellect" and that education was to filter down from them to the masses.

Acceptance of Minute by Lord William Bentinck: Lord William Bentinck endorsed the Minute by writing one line beneath it, "I give my entire concurrence to the sentiments expressed in the Minute". He passed the Resolution of march, 1835 which determined the aim, content and medium of instruction in India.

APPRAISAL OF MACAULAY'S MINUTE : WAS HE THE TORCH BEARER OR EVIL GENIUS?

Macaulay's intentions become very clear with his following statements:

Religious Fanaticism: In a letter to his father in 1836, Macaulay wrote, "Our English schools are increasing with leaps and bounds and now the condition has reached to a position that it has become difficult to accommodate the students. Hindus are much influenced with education. There is no Hindu who may keep real faith in his religion after studying English. I have full confidence that if our education policy succeeds, then no idolator will be left in Bengal. All this will be done naturally, without any religious preaching and interference."

On July 10, 1837, Macaulay expressed the following views before the House of Commons in England, "It may be that the public mind of India may expand under our system that having instructed in European languages, they may in some future age demand European institutions. Whether such a day will ever come I know not. Whenever it comes it will be the proudest day in English history."

That Macaulay was the torch bearer is an exaggerated claim. Lord Macaulay was not the first person who pleaded the cause of Western Education and inspired the Indian people with ideas. He was also not the founder of Orientalist or Anglicist group as such groups had already been working before his arrival in the country. He, of course, ended the controversy and gave a new direction to the system of education in India. To quote S.N. Mukerji, "Macaulay simply took the tide of popular opinion at its flood that had been running high through the spade work done by Raja Rammohan Roy." Again according to him, "Macaulay tried to grow a temperate plant on warm plains of equatorial region, where it was possible for it to survive under artificial circumstance but not to thrive."

Nurullah and Naik do not call Lord Macaulay as the torchbearer in the path of progress though they admit Macaulay's contribution in this respect.

S.N. Mukerji has given a balanced appraisal of Macaulay's Minutes. "Macaulay's Minutes had all the defects of a preliminary spadework, but it is a very important document, because it influenced Britain's educational policy in this country for more than a century. It should be admitted that Western learning has done good to India, and better results have been achieved through Macaulay's bold policy than it would have been possible through half-hearted attempts of the Orientalists. The new knowledge led to India's unity and her great recovery brought her into contact with scientific research of the West and developed Indian languages to a standard in which a university education became possible. But his Minutes can neither be regarded as the Greater Charter of Indian Education nor it can be condemned as the evil genius of Macaulay.

Net Result of Macaulay's Minute

Merits

1. A clear-cut picture of the national system of education in India emerged.
2. The system proved very helpful in promoting the objectives for which it was planned.
3. English schools began to be established.
4. English became the medium of instruction.
5. Western arts and sciences became popular.
6. Filtration theory of Education emerged.

Demerits

1. Indian culture and philosophy receded to the background.
2. Vernacular languages began to be neglected.

3. Mass education was neglected.
4. Western culture made rapid strives.
5. Arabic and Sanskrit languages found very few takers.
6. Arabic, Maktabs and Sanskrit Pathshalas saw gradual disappearance.

ACCEPTANCE OF MACAULAY'S MINUTE AND LORD WILLIAM BENTINCK'S RESOLUTION OF MARCH 7, 1835.

The Minute of Lord Macaulay 1835 was accepted by Lord William Bentinck (1828-1835). He endorsed it by writing one line beneath it, "I give my entire concurrence to the sentiments expressed in the minute." The Resolution of March 1835 eventually determined the aim, content and medium of instruction in India. Promotion of western sciences and arts was acknowledged as the avowed object of the British Government in India.

Resolution

First, His Lordship-in-Council is of the opinion that the great object of the British Government ought to be the promotion of European literature and science among the natives of India; and that all the funds appropriate from the purpose of education would be best employed on English education alone.

Second, but it is not the intention of His Lordship-in-Council to abolish any college or school of native learning, while the native population shall appear to be inclined to avail themselves of the advantages which it affords, and His Lordship-in-Council directs that all the existing professors and students at all institutions under the superintendence of the Committee shall continue to receive their stipends ... no stipend shall be given to any student that may hereafter enter at any of these institutions; and that when any professor of oriental learning shall vacate his situation, the Committee shall report to the Government the number and state of the class in order that the government may be able to decide upon the expediency of appointing a successor.

Third, it has come to the knowledge of the Governor General-in-Council that a large sum has been expended by the committee on the printing of oriental works; His Lordship-in-Council directs that no portion of the funds shall hereafter be so employed.

Fourth, His Lordship-in-Council directs that all the funds which these reforms will leave at the disposal of the Committee be henceforth employed in imparting to the native population a knowledge of English literature and science through the medium of the English language; and His Lordship-in-Council requests the Committee to submit to government with all expedition, a plan for the accomplishment of this purpose.

Evaluation of Bentinck's Proclamation

Bentinck's proclamation was the first declaration of the educational policy of the British Government which it wanted to adopt in this country. Bentinck was greatly influenced by the views of Macaulay. The Orientalists lost their battle. With Bentinck's proclamation the following results were clearly visible:

1. The aims of education in India were defined by the British.
2. Type of education envisaged for Indian people was spelt out.
3. The promotion of Western arts and sciences was acknowledged as the avowed object.
4. The printing of oriental works was to be stopped.
5. New grants or stipends to students of oriental institutions were to be stopped in future.
6. The proclamation promised to supply Government with English educated Indian servants cheap but capable at the same time.

7. The proclamation accelerated the growth of new learning by leaps and bounds.

S.N. Mukerji has analysed the results of Bentinck's proclamation as, "The proclamation marks a turning point in the history of education in India. It was the first declaration of the educational policy, which, the British Government wanted to adopt in this country. ...The barriers of caste, conservatism and religious orthodoxy which had blocked the cultural progress of the country were done away with and new vistas were opened through the study of English for those persons 'Indian in blood and colour but English in tastes, in opinions, in morals and in intellect'. This brought about the dawn of a cultural renaissance after centuries of confusion and darkness."

DOWNWARD FILTRATION THEORY OF EDUCATION

The British rulers in India thought that in order to run the administration peacefully and smoothly it was essential to make the higher classes blind followers of the Britishers. This they wanted to achieve through educating the classes. This theory meant "Education is to be filtered to the common people. Drop by drop, the education would go to the common public so that at due time it may take the form of a vast stream which remained water desert of the society starved for water for a long time and high class of people would be educated and common people would gain influence from them."

"Education was to permeate from above. Drop by drop from the Himalayas of Indian life useful information was to trickle downwards forming in a time a broad and steady stream to irrigate the thirsty plains."

Reasons for the Adoption of Filtration Theory

1. The British rulers needed various types of employees to run the business and the Government. They wanted

educated persons for this. So they started the policy of educating higher classes.

2. The Government did not have sufficient funds for educating the masses.
3. The educated people educated on British lines through English medium would get higher posts in Government services and then naturally they would use their influence in controlling the masses from going against the Government rule.
4. Higher classes educated through the medium of English would adopt English ways and in turn influence the lower classes.
5. After educating some people, the responsibility of educating the masses could be left to them.

Background of the Adoption of Filtration Theory

The Directors of the Company had written in their Dispatch, dated 29 September 1830, to Madras Government: "The improvements in education, however, which most effectually contribute to elevate the moral and intellectual condition of a people are those, which concern the education of the higher classes of the persons possessing leisure and natural influence over minds of their countrymen. By raising the standard of education among these classes you would eventually produce a much greater and more beneficial change in the ideas and feelings of the community than you can hope to produce by acting directly on the more numerous class."

Lord Macaulay had ideas similar to those of the Directors of the Company. In his Minute of 1835, he has said, "At present we should create such group of people who may work as a mediator between us and the common people, a class of persons, Indians in blood and colour, but English in tastes, in opinions, in morals and in intellect. It will be their duty to develop the native languages and enable it to convey the knowledge to the common people." Again on 31st July, 1837, he said: "At present we don't aim at educating directly the common people. We aim at creating a class of persons, who among their countrymen distribute some of the knowledge we gave."

The Committee of Public Instruction in Bengal had also approved the same ideal and expressed its ideas in 1839, "Our efforts should be concentrated first on the education of higher and middle class of people". Sir Auckland had also accepted this view and declaring it as Government policy, he said, "The Government should educate the higher class of the people so that the 'Filtered culture' reaches to the public." Since then this policy was followed upto 1870 and emphasis was laid on the education of the people of higher classes in the society.

Evaluation of the Filtration theory

The immediate aim of getting educated people to run the various jobs in the administration was fully achieved. It also helped in creating a faithful class of people. It settled the educational policy of the British rulers and education began to progress rapidly.

The ultimate aim could not be fulfilled as the educated persons were cut off from the common masses. The common masses began to look upon the educated classes as the favoured children of the British Government. The higher and richer classes began to copy British food, taste, behaviour and manners. Their entire daily routine was westernised. They became more and more self-centred and a great cleavage was created between the rich and the poor.

ORIENTAL — ANGLICIST OR OCCIDENTAL CONTROVERSY ON THE SYSTEM OF EDUCATION IN INDIA AND MACAULAY'S MINUTE

When the East India company embarked on its political conquests in India in 1757, there was no education system organised and supported by the State. Gradually it was realised by the rulers to take interest in education. In 1813, the Company decided to spend a sum of Rs. One lakh on education in India.

This led to Oriental-Anglicist controversy on education.

Oriental Print of View: This school of thought wanted to encourage the indigenous system of education in India and wanted the Company to spend the amount on the promotion of this system. Among the important supporters of this policy were: Warren Hastings, H.T. Princep, Lord Minto, Charles Grant and H.H. William. The Anglicists found their supporter in Lord Macaulay who translated their dream into reality to a considerable extent. Raja Rammohan Roy (1772-1833), a distinguished Indian educationist, religious and social reformers appreciated the merits of western philosophy and science and was an ardent supporter of the educational reforms advocated by the Anglicists.

Charles Grant who had been associated with the East India Company's administration in London and Calcutta believed that Britain had a mission of regenerating Hindu society pleaded that 'She (Britain) must do so through the English language'. He further observed, "The Hindus erred because they were ignorant. This darkness could be dispelled by the introduction of Christianity and the art and sciences of Europe."

Trevelyan wrote in '*On the Education of the Education of the People of India*' as "The spirit of English literature cannot be but favourable to the English connection". English education would stop the Indians from regarding their rulers as foreigners and in fact would make them "intelligent and zealous cooperators".

ADAM'S REPORTS ON EDUCATION

Brief Life Sketch of William Adam (1789-1868). A Christian priest of Scotland, William Adam came to India in 1818 and spent about 27 years here. He came into contact with Raja Rammohan Roy and both of them influenced each other. He was greatly impressed by Indian views regarding the existence of one Almighty God. In due course he renounced Christian priesthood.

Period Covered in Adam's Report on Education

Lord William Bentinck, the Governor-General of India appointed Adam in 1835 to survey the state of education in Bengal and Bihar and to suggest reforms. Adam submitted three reports (1835-1838). His first report was a digest of the earlier reports on the subjects. The second and the third reports were based on the survey he conducted. The second report was a thorough enquiry on the system of education prevalent in Natlore, in the district of Rajshahi. The third report covers five districts of Bengal and Bihar and his recommendations for the reforms of indigenous schools.

Contents of the Reports

First Report

The following paragraph of the report has led to a good deal of controversy.

"Indigenous Elementary Schools : By this description are meant those schools in which instruction in the elements of knowledge is communicated, and which have been originated and are supported by religion or philanthropic societies. The number of such schools in Bengal is supposed to be very great. A distinguished member of the General Committee of Public Instruction in a Minute on the subject expressed the opinion, that if one rupee per mensem were expended on each existing village school in the Lower Provinces, the amount would probably fall little short of lakhs of rupees per annum. This supposes that there are 100,000 such schools in Bengal and Bihar and assuming the population of these two provinces to be 40,000,000, there would be a village school for every 400 persons."

Observations on the First Report

While scholars like Sir Philip Hartig dubhed the report as a 'myth', scholars like R.V. Parulekar considered this report substantially a 'reality'. The chief point of different opinions revolved round the term 'school'. Sir Philip Hartig considered the term school as an institution in the modern sense with its own structure and number of students of the locality who in return paid fees and other perquisites and or the remuneration was paid by the community. According to the other view a school was a place where instruction was given to one student or more students either by the teacher or the father himself or any member of the family.

Adam's Second Report

Adam's second report covered Naltore Thana, in district Rajshahi with a population of 129,640 Muslims and 65,656 Hindus. There were two types of schools, i.e., regular schools, similar to modern schools and domestic schools or schools where family members taught or a teacher was employed to teach. As against 27 elementary schools and 262 students, there were nearly 2360, i.e., nearly nine times students in domestic schools. Following were the important findings:

Age of Schooling: The average age of admission to an elementary school was 8 years and the average school leaving age was 14 years.

Schools for the Teaching of Quran: There were 11 Arabic schools for this purpose.

Type of Elementary Schools: There were 10 Bengali schools, and 4 Persian schools.

Average Number of Students in a School: The average number of students in a school was 10.

Average Pay of the Teacher: Pay ranged between Rs.5-8 per month.

Female Education: Female education was non-existent.

Literacy Rate: Literacy percentage was 6.1 percent. Total literary percentage of males and females was 3.1

Indigenous Colleges: There was no indigenous college conducted by Muslims. There were 38 Sanskrit Colleges with 397 students.

Table 1.1: Educational Facilities in India According to Adam

A. Schools

District	Number of schools								Total
	Bengali	Hindi	Sanskrit	Persian	Formal Arabic	Arabic	English	Girls	
Murshidabad	62	5	24	17	—	2	2	1	113
Birbhum	407	5	56	71	—	2	2	1	544
Burdwan	629+1 (infants)	—	190	93	3	8	3	4	931
South Bihar	—	86	27	279	—	12	1	—	605
Tirhut	—	80	56	234	—	4	—	—	374
Total	1,099	376	353		3	28	8	6	2,567

B. Scholars

District	Number of scholars					Total
	Bengali & Hindi	Sanskrit	Persian & Arabic	English	Girls	
Murshidabad	1,080	153	109	26	28	1,396
Birbhum	6,383	393	490	73	11	7,350
Burdwan	13,190	1,358	971	120	175	15,814
South Bihar	3,090	437	1,486	23	—	5,036
Tirhut	507	214	598	—	—	1,319
Total	24,250	2,555	3,654	242	214	30,915

These statistics *exclude* the centres of domestic instruction.

Fees etc. in Colleges: Food, lodging and education was free in colleges.

Adam's Third Report

Adam's Third Report is divided into two parts. The first part covers educational data collected by him for five districts, viz., Murshidabad, Birbhum, Burdwan, South Bihar and Tirhut. The second part provides proposals put forward by Adams for the reform of education, especially indigenous.

Methods of Collection of Data and Accuracy of the Data: Adam followed two methods. One, he himself collected information from one *'Thana'* of each district. Second, his agents collected data from all other *'Thanas'*.

In the conduct of the survey, two difficulties were encountered with. One related to means of travel and communication and the other related to the various types of suspicions among the people regarding the motive of survey.

Table 1.2: Educational Facilities as Given by Sir Philip Hartog

Area	*Population*	*No. of schools actually existing*	*Hypothetical number of schools on the basis of one school per 400 of population*
Murshidabad	186,841	113	467
Birbhum	1,267,067	544	3,168
Burdwan	1,187,580	931	2,969
South Bihar	1,340,610	605	3,352
Tirhut	1,697,700	374	4,244

Some Aspects of Indian Education. Sir Philip Hartog

General Features of Indigenous Education as Observed by Adam

Types and Agencies Related to Schools

Adam classified different educational agencies into seven categories.

1. Indigenous elementary schools.

2. Elementary schools not indigenous, i.e., new types of elementary schools run by missionaries and others.
3. Domestic education.
4. English schools.
5. Native female schools.
6. Indigenous schools for advanced learning (colleges).
7. Adult instruction.

Extent of Education: Adam says that no village in Bengal was without a primary school. There were about one lakh of schools scattered in all the villages. Adam called schools as the places and homes where education was given.

Teacher's Salary: Teachers were paid Rs. 5 to 8 per month.

Duration of Schooling: The students started education at the age of 8 and read up to the age of 14 years.

Courses of Studies: The Hindus were generally reading Bengali and Sanskrit and Muslims were reading Arabic and Persian.

Education of Women: Adam states that the very name of women education made people afraid.

Schools Open for All: Schools were not meant for a particular caste or class of society. They were open to every one who wanted to study.

Measures for Reforming the System

1. Publication of a graded series of new textbooks (I-IV) in Bengali, Hindi and Urdu, to be prepared by Indians and Europeans in collaboration.
2. Appointment of an examiner for each district. It was suggested that the examiner should survey his area, supply and explain textbooks to teachers, examine teachers on the content of textbooks already provided after a period of six months, distribute grants and record to teachers according to the percentage or passes in school examinations, and supervise the work of teachers.

3. Appointment of inspectors for supervising the work of examines.
4. Training of teachers. Adam proposed to convert Vernacular Departments of English schools into normal schools for training teachers of indigenous schools. He suggested that these teachers should be required to study in these schools for three months in a year for four successive years.
5. Award of small grants of land to village schools for their maintenance.
6. Organisation of experimental farms for agricultural education.

Evaluation of Adam's Recommendations

Adam's recommendations were not accepted by the Government. Before he submitted his third Report, Macaulay as the Chairman of the Committee had pronounced his verdict. Macaulay was wedded to the Filtration theory and believed firmly in the superiority of western civilisation. According to Macaulay, indigenous schools were useless. He observed, "I am little inclined to doubt, however, whether we are at present ripe for any extensive practical measure, which he (Adam) recommends. Our work is to educate the school masters for the next generation." The Committee regarded Adam's plan as impractical and accepted the views of Macaulay. Adam submitted his resignation.

F.W. Thomas thinks, "From the accuracy of its information, the candour, sense and statesmanship of its author (Adam) it is among the most valuable and interesting publication on education in India." S.N. Mukerji regards Adam's Reports "as one of the ablest reports ever written on Indian education" and he laments on the fate of this report. "A golden opportunity for building up a national system of education, based on culture and languages of the people, was thus lost."

INDIGENOUS SYSTEM OF EDUCATION IN INDIA AT THE BEGINNING OF THE BRITISH RULE IN INDIA

A Well-Developed System

Following statements illustrate the state of indigenous system of education:

1. 'An officer of Colonel Baillie's Detachment' renders a beautiful picture of indigenous educational institutions of the Hindus. This picture will be a very pleasing one, particularly for those who wail that the depressed classes were denied education as if it was the reserved pasture for caste-Hindus. "Even the inferior classes are taught reading, writing and arithmetics. The youth are taught not within the door, but in the open air, and it is a singular, but not unpleasing spectacle to behold, in every village, a venerable old man reclined on a terraced plain teaching a number of surrounding boys, who regard him with the utmost reverence. In the simple seminaries, where the want of magnificent and tractable sons of Hindus are not only prepared for the business but induced in the duties of life; a profound veneration for the objects of religious worship; reverence of their parents; respect for their seniors, justice and humanity towards all men but a particular Hindu for those of their own caste. The Hindi language is beautiful, expressive. In reading and speaking, the Hindus are very musical". (*Memoirs of the Late War in Asia*, J. Murray, London, 1787, Vol. II, pp. 228-230). "There is wonderful mildness in their manners and also in their laws, which are influenced by their manners" (*ibid* p. 233).
2. The following remarkable statement was made by Mr. G.L. Prendergast, a member of the Bombay Governor's Council in his Minute of 1821:

   I need hardly mention what every member of the Board knows as well as I do, that there is hardly a village, great or small, throughout our territories, in which there is not at least one school, and in larger villages more, many in every town and in larger cities in every division; where young natives are taught reading, writing and arithmetic, upon a system so economical, from a handful or two of grain, to perhaps a rupee per month to the school master; according to the ability of the parents, and at the same time so simple and effectual that there is hardly a cultivator or petty dealer who is not competent to keep his own accounts with a degree of accuracy, in my opinion, beyond what we meet with amongst the lower orders in our own country; while the more spending dealers and bankers keep their books with a degree of cease, conciseness and clearness, I rather think fully equal to those of any British Merchant (Evidence of 1832, p. 468).

3. There are schools maintained by the natives in almost every village in Candeish (Evidence of 1832, p. 296).
4. There are probably as great proportion of persons in India who can read, write and keep simple accounts as are to be found in European Countries [Fifth Annual Report (1819) of the Bombay Education Society, p. 11].
   Source: R.V. Parulekar, *A Source Book of History of Education in the Bombay Province*, part I, Survey of Indigenous Education (1820-30). Quoted by Syed Nurullah and J.P. Naik in *A Students' History of Education in India* (1800-1965). Macmillan and Co. Limited, Bombay, 1964.
5. The state of education low as it is compared with that of our country, is higher than it was in most European countries at not very distant period. It has, no doubt, been better in earlier period. (Sir Thomas Munro's Enquiry in Madras, July 1922).
6. The elementary system was intended for the masses. It was widespread system consisting of numerous primary

schools scattered all over the countryside. Practically every village has its primary school.
(*'Education in Modern India'*, A.N. Basu).

7. At the beginning of the 19th century, there existed a fairly wide spread organisation of primary education in most parts of India.

Primary Education in Madras

1. *Extent*: Each village in Madras had a primary school. In some of the districts the average number of students per school was about 120. Some people used to educate their children at home. Most of the students were Hindus. Very few of the girls entered the school.
2. *Courses*: Most of the schools provided education in provincial schools. There was no uniformity of courses. Primary schools in general taught arithmetic, reading of scriptures, fine stories and beautiful poems.
3. *Duration of Schooling*: Generally boys of well-to-do classes started going to school at the age of five and continued their studies upto the age of 14 or 15 years.
4. *Ceremony While Starting Studies*: 'Havan' and 'Ganesh Pujan' were performed to which the kith and kin of the boy were invited. Afterwards the 'Guru' caused the boy recite the prayer of 'Ganeshji'. The parents of the boy gave 'Dakshina' (gift) to 'Guru.
5. *Daily Routine*: Routine was same for the students. The school used to start at about 6 with 'Saraswati Vandana, i.e., prayer of goddess of learning.
6. *School Discipline*: Discipline was very hard. Guilty students were severely caned.
7. *Methods of Teaching*: Students started writing the alphabets on sand or ground with their fingers. Afterwards they started writing on small wooden planks, i.e., Patti and chalk and pen of wood (Kalam).

8. *Monitorial System*: The teachers used monitorial system. Good students of higher classes were given chance to teach the students of lower classes.
9. *Salary of Teachers*: Teachers were mostly ill paid. Their pay could hardly feed them.

Primary Education in Bombay

1. *School Buildings*: There were no separate school buildings. Education was carried on in temples, houses of teachers and residences of respectable persons.
2. *Number of Schools*: There was at least one school in every village. The average number of student per school was fifteen. The highest number in a school was 150.
3. *Fees*: Teachers were paid 'Sidha', one rupee per month by the guardians of a student.
4. *Courses of Study*: Students were taught to read, write and do ordinary and practical arithmetic. They were made to learn, by heart the 'Pahara' and 'Ginti' (counting of numbers etc.).
5. *Duration*: Students started schooling at the age of 6 and continued upto the age of 14 years.
6. *Discipline*: Hard punishments were generally given to the students for not maintaining discipline and learning lessons.
7. *Status and Conditions of Teachers*: They did not teach from economic point of view. Generally they were Brahmans but sometimes Marathas, Bhandaris and Vaishyas were also working as teachers. They were generally invited at festivals and received some gifts and presents on particular occasions. As a tradition, they got 3 to 5 rupees per month.

Elphinstone's Minute (1823)

The famous educational minute of Elphinstone, dated the 13th December 1823 suggested the following seven measures:

1. to improve the mode of teaching at native schools and to increase the number of schools;
2. to supply them with school books;
3. to hold out some encouragement to the lower orders of natives to avail themselves of the means of instruction;
4. to establish schools for teaching the European sciences and improvements in the higher branches of education;
5. to provide for the preparation and publication of books of moral and physical science in native languages;
6. to establish schools for the purpose of teaching English to those disposed to pursue it as a classical language and as a means of acquiring a knowledge of European discoveries;
7. to hold forth encouragement to the natives in the pursuit of those lost branches of knowledge.

All these proposals were not accepted by the Council. This minute was violently opposed by Mr. Francis Warden, a member of the Council. The difference of opinion gave rise to Anglo-Vernacular controversy. As a result of this Minute, however, many vernacular schools were opened.

Early Missionary Schools

There is no doubt that the early Christian missionaries played an important role in the spread of education in India. It is sometimes alleged that the main motive was to promote Christianity.

Portuguese Missionaries: Among the Europeans, Portuguese missionaries were the first to start educational institutions in India. The main centres of their work were Bombay, Goa, Daman, Diu, Chittagong and Hugli. Those who followed Christianity were given free education. The children of the poor Christians were also given free food, books, etc. The name of St. Francis Xavier who came to India in 1542 is associated with many institutions even today.

Dutch Missionaries: Dutch missionaries did not make their educational institutions as centres of religious propaganda. Their educational institutions did not survive for long as they could not compete with the Britishers in supremacy over India.

French Missionaries: The missionaries started their schools at Pondicherry, Mahi, Yaman and Karaikal but in due course these schools were taken over by the English when they took possession of these territories.

Danes: Danish religious preachers started schools for boys who became Christians and they were taught Tamil. They also started a training college for teachers in Travancore. Schools were also started in Madras Fort William, St. David, Trichrapalli and Tanjore where English was also taught, besides other subjects.

Characteristics of Early Mission Schools

Following were the striking features of early mission schools.

1. Religious instruction according to the tenets of Christianity was compulsory and the Bible was used as a class-book.
2. The curriculum was wide and included subjects like grammar, history and geography.
3. Printed textbooks were also introduced.
4. Classes were held regularly at fixed hours. Sunday was a holiday.

2

Wood's Despatch (1854) and Indian Education Commission (1882)

NOMENCLATURE OF WOOD'S DESPATCH

Wood's Despatch derives its name from Sir Charles Wood who was the President of the Board of Control for India. The Despatch is an important policy document on education containing 100 clauses. It contained definite aims of education and directions for the implementation of education policy in India. The Despatch was prepared by three eminent English thinkers, namely, Marshman, Parry and Wilson. They made an intensive study of the problems of education and thereafter prepared the scheme of education.

CIRCUMSTANCES LEADING TO WOOD'S DESPATCH

The Charter Act of the East India Company was to be reviewed in 1853 by the British Parliament. Before doing so, the Parliament wanted to examine the entire working of the Company. This also implied an evaluation of the education policy followed by the Company in India. So the British Parliament appointed a Special Parliamentary Committee to suggest a suitable educational policy for India.

ESSENCE OF THE REPORT : POLICY DECLARATION

Following extracts from the report provide the essence of the report and the policy declaration.

The Despatch observed, "The system of science and philosophy which forms the learning of the East abounds with grave errors, and Eastern literature is at best very deficient as regards all modern discovery and improvement"; and concluded the discussion with the following declaration:

"We must emphatically declare that the education which we were desire to see extended in India is that which has for its object the diffusion of the improved arts, science, philosophy and literature of Europe; in short, of European knowledge."

MAIN RECOMMENDATIONS/POLICY DECISIONS

1. *Objectives of the Educational Policy*: The Despatch had the following objectives in view:

(a) To confer upon the natives of India those vast and material blessings which flow from the general diffusion of Western knowledge;
(b) Not only to produce a high degree of intellectual fitness but also to raise the moral character of those who partake of the above advantages;
(c) To supply the East India Company with reliable and capable public servants; and
(d) To secure for England a large and more certain supply of many articles, necessary for her manufactures and extensively consumed by her population, as well as an almost inexhaustible demand for the produce of British labour.

2. *Medium of Instruction: English and Vernacular Languages*: In any general system of education, English language should be taught where there is a demand for it; but such instruction should always be combined with a careful attention to the study of the vernacular language of the district, and with such general instruction as can be conveyed through that language; and while the English language continues to be made use of as by

far the most perfect medium for the education of those persons who have acquired a sufficient knowledge of it to receive general instruction through it, the vernacular languages must be employed to teach the far larger classes who are ignorant, of or imperfectly acquainted with English.

3. *Translation of English Literature*: At the same time, and as the importance of the vernacular languages becomes more appreciated, the vernacular literature of India would be gradually enriched by translations of European books or by the original compositions of men whose minds have been imbued with the spirit of European advancement, so that European knowledge may gradually be placed in this manner within the reach of all classes of the people.

4. *Grant-in-Aid – Transfer of Government Institutions to the Local Bodies*: We look forward to the time when any general system of education entirely provided by Government may be discontinued, with the gradual advance of the system of grant-in-aid, and when many of the existing Government institutions, especially those of the higher order, may be safely closed or transferred to the management of local bodies under the control of and aided by the State.

5. *Voluntary Religious Education in Government Institutions*: The Despatch observed, "Considerable misapprehension appears to exist as to our views with respect to religious instruction in the Government institutions. Such instruction being entirely voluntary on both sides, it is necessary, in order to prevent the slightest suspicion of an intention on our part to make use of the influence of Government for the purpose of proselytism, that no notice shall be taken of it by the inspectors in their periodical visits."

6. *Training of Teachers*: For securing properly qualified teachers the Despatch observed "We cannot do better than refer you to the plan which has been adopted in Great Britain for this subject, and which appears to us to be capable of easy adaptation to India. It mainly consists in the selection and

stipend of pupil-teachers (awarding a small payment to the masters of the school in which they are employed for the instruction out of school hours); their ultimate removal, if they prove worthy, to normal school; the issue to them of certificates on the completion of their training in those normal schools; and in securing to them a sufficient salary when they are afterwards employed as school masters. This system should be carried out in India, both in the Government colleges and schools, and, by means of grant-in-aid, in all institutions which are brought under Government inspection..."

7. *Status of Teachers*: "Our wish is that the profession of school master may, for the future, afford inducements to the natives of India such as are held out in other branches of the public service."

8. *Education of Women*: The Despatch stressed the importance of female education and stated, "The importance of female education in India cannot be over-rated; and we have observed with pleasure the evidence which is now afforded of an increased desire on the part of many of the natives of India to give a good education to their daughters. By this means a far greater proportional impulse is imparted to the educational and moral tone of the people than by the education of men. We have already observed that schools for females are included among those to which grants-in-aid may be given; and we cannot refrain from expressing our cordial sympathy with the efforts which are being made in this direction.

9. *Establishment of Universities*: "The rapid spread of a liberal education among the natives of India since that time, the high attainments shown by the native candidates for Government scholarship and by native students in private institutions, in their success in the Medical Colleges, and the requirement of an increasing European and Anglo-Indian population, have led us to the conclusion that the time is now arrived for the establishment of universities in India."

10. *Expansion of Mass Education*: "Our attention should be

directed, to a consideration, if possible still more important and one which hitherto, we are bound to admit to, much neglected namely how useful and practical knowledge, suited to every walk of life, may be best conveyed to the great mass of the people."

MERITS OF THE DESPATCH

1. It clearly laid down the educational policy.
2. It made the Government responsible for education.
3. It gave directions in almost all areas of education ad at various levels.
4. It accepted the importance of Indian culture, literature and philosophy.
5. It prepared the blue-print of the administrative set up of education.
6. It gave due importance to vernacular languages.
7. It recognised the utility of indigenous schools.
8. It formulated a definite grant-in-aid policy.
9. It stressed the importance of training of teachers.
10. It pointed out the necessity of raising the salary of teachers.
11. It made provision for providing stipends to the poor and deserving students.
12. It drew attention to women education.
13. It emphasised vocational education.
14. It gave due importance to mass education.
15. It emphasised the need for opening universities in India.

DEMERITS AND SHORTCOMINGS OF THE DESPATCH

1. It glorified western knowledge at the cost of Indian culture and philosophy.
2. It encouraged the spread of English as it recommended that the newly educated persons would be given preference in government services.

3. Religious education which was an integral part of indigenous education was discouraged.
4. It reflected a soft attitude towards Christian missionaries.
5. Grant-in-aid system was defective. Those institutions that could not raise 50 percent of their own resources were not eligible for grant.
6. Education became an instrument for passing examination for the sole purpose of securing a job.
7. Bureaucracy became supreme in the running of the educational system.
8. Foreign university pattern came into vogue.
9. Bookish knowledge was encouraged.

IMPACT OF WOOD'S DESPATCH

1. By and large, recommendations of Wood's Despatch were adopted.
2. Departments of Public Instruction (Education Departments) were abolished in all provinces.
3. There was increase in grant-in-aid.
4. Religious neutrality in education was observed.
5. Professional education was encouraged.

Three years after Wood's Despatch, there was the 1857 Revolt which brought about far-reaching changes in the political scenario of India.

EVALUATION OF THE DESPATCH: VIEWS OF EDUCATIONISTS

1. According to *Nurullah and Naik*, "The Despatch of 1854 was at first looked upon as the beginning of a great era of educational reforms under the East India Company. But, as events actually turned out, it proved to be its swan song ... The Company ceased to be a political power in 1858 and the Government of India came directly under the crown. Broadly

speaking, therefore, education in India under the East India Company may be taken to have ended with the Despatch of 1854 itself."

Regarding Despatch's impact on education, Nurullah and Naik have made the following observations:

One. The plans of mass education visualised by the Despatch were not realised.

Second. High schools imparting education through the medium of mother-tongue were established only after more then seven decades.

Third. One was pained to find that the Despatch could only think of India as the supplier of raw materials for the British industries and as the consumer of the finished products of England. Such a position could hardly be accepted by any self-respecting Indian either from the economic or educational point of view.

Notwithstanding this criticism of the Despatch, the authors appreciated that the Despatch did a lot towards the evolution of a good system of education in India according to educational ideals then prevalent.

2. *Prof. S.N. Mukerjee* observes in his book '*History of Education in India*', "The Despatch is indeed a very important document and James considers it to be the 'Magna Charta' of English Education in India". It was the first authoritative declaration on the part of the British Parliament about the educational policy to be followed in India. It was admitted that the education of the people is the duty of the State. The Despatch is so comprehensive in its nature that Indian educationists have not yet succeeded in fulfilling the tasks which it had set. It provided a scheme, which was tried us to the university stage. It partially recognised the value of Indian culture, and at the same time it showed the need for grafting European knowledge on it. The Despatch rightly defined the comparative position of English and Indian Languages in a general scheme of education for this country."

3. *Lord Dalhousie* declared that Despatch contained "a scheme of education for all India, far wider and more comprehensive than the Local or the Supreme Government could have ever ventured to suggest."

4. *H.R. James* observes, "The Despatch of 1854 is thus the climax in the history of Indian education; what goes before leads up to it, what follows from it."

5. *Prof. A.N. Basu* has opined "The Despatch is said to be the corner-stone of Indian education. It is said to have laid foundations of our present system of education."

THE DESPATCH — A MAGNA CHARTA OF EDUCATION OR NOT

The term Magna Charta denotes an official document or policy which bestows or guarantees certain rights and privileges. A perusal of the various provisions contained in the Despatch does not provide any evidence for calling it a Magna Charta of education. It fell short of expectations. The authors of the Despatch did not aim at education for leadership. It failed to provide for any plan for the Industrial regeneration of India. In fact it visualised India as a market for the supplier of raw materials to Britain and a consumer market for the purchase of finished goods of Britain's industries. Thus, its vocational policy was lopsided. Accordingly, it neglected the all round development of the individuals. The Despatch did not refer to the ideal of universal literacy. It did not recognise the obligation of the state to educate every child before a certain age. Nevertheless Despatch was an important educational document in the then prevailing situation. It would not be quite relevant to compare the Despatch with the Scenario of the 21st century. The Despatch has to be evaluated in the context of the 19th century. It was meant to serve the ends of the British rulers. Thus it was neither a Magna Charta nor a document without any utility. It must be admitted that since 1757, it was the most outstanding document on education.

Wood's Despatch was of great significance. For the first time a comprehensive scheme which touched the education on various vital points was presented.

INDIAN EDUCATION COMMISSION OR HUNTER COMMISSION (1882)

Circumstances Leading to the Appointment of the Indian Education Commission

As a result of Wood's Despatch, universities were established in 1857 by different Acts at Calcutta, Bombay and Madras on the pattern of the London University. Lahore University was established in 1869. There was a rapid growth of colleges. Besides Government colleges, numerous private institutions also sprang up. These universities considered that university examinations were designed for the male sex only. It was only in 1877 that the Calcutta University threw the matriculation examination open to girls. This was followed by Madras in 1881 and Bombay in 1883. It was felt that too much was being done in India for higher education and that primary education was being neglected. The Government did not carry out the grant-in-aid policy as suggested by the Wood's Despatch. The missionaries were hit hard by such a policy as they were managing a number of English schools and colleges. When the agitation of the missionaries did not bear fruit in India, they started an organisation in London which was known as the General Council of Education in India (1878). As a result of the agitation raised by the Council in London, Lord Ripon appointed the first Indian Education Commission on February 3, 1882, with Sir William Hunter (Member of Viceroy's Executive Council) as Chairman and twenty others as members.

The Commission is sometimes called as 'Hunter Commission' after the name of its Chairman. The Commission included 20 members besides the president. The Government accepted all the recommendations of the Commission except those in connection with religious education.

Terms of Reference of the Commission

1. It will be the duty of the Commission to enquire particularly into the manner in which effect has been given to the principles of the Despatch of 1854; and to suggest such measures as it may think desirable in order to the further carrying out of the policy therein laid down.
2. It is the desire of the Governor General-in-Council that the Commission should specially bear in mind the great importance which the Government attaches to the subjects of primary education. The development of elementary education was the main object contemplated by the Despatch of 1854 ...; the principal object, therefore, of the enquiry of the Commission should be the present state of elementary education throughout the Empire and the means by which this can everywhere be extended and improved.

Specific Issues before the Commission

(a) Should Government withdraw from direct educational enterprise in favour of missionaries, as the Despatch of 1854 had led some of them to hope?

(b) What should be the policy of Government on religious education? Should it be imparted in schools or not? If it was to be imparted, in what form and subject and on what conditions was it to be allowed?

Important Recommendations

I. Encouragement to Indigenous Education

Admitting, ... however, the comparative inferiority of indigenous institutions, we consider that efforts should now be made to encourage them. They have survived a severe competition, and have thus proved that they possess both vitality and popularity.

II. Primary Education

Importance of Primary Education: The Commission observed, "That while every branch of education can justly claim the fostering care of the State, it is desirable, in the present circumstances of the country, to declare the elementary education of the masses, its provision, extension and improvement to be that part of the educational system to which the strenuous efforts of the State should now be directed in a still larger measure than heretofore.

That primary education be declared to be that part of the whole system of public instruction, which possesses an almost exclusive claim on local funds set apart for education, and a large claim on provincial revenues.

We recommend that supply of normal schools whether Government or aided, be so localised as to provide for the local requirements of all primary schools whether Government or aided, within the division under each Inspector."

Recommendations on Primary Education

The Commission gave considerable attention to primary education and their recommendations can be conveniently divided under the following heads:

1. Policy;
2. Legislation and administration;
3. Encouragement of indigenous schools;
4. School curriculum; and
5. Finance.

1. *Policy*. Regarding the policy of Government towards primary education, the Commission recommended:

(i) That primary education be regarded as the instruction of the masses through the vernacular in such subjects as will fit them for their position in life, and be not necessarily regarded as a portion of instruction leading upto the university.

(ii) That while every branch of education can justly claim

the fostering care of the State, it is desirable, in the present circumstances of the country, to declare the elementary education of the masses, its provision, extension, and improvement, to be that part of the education system to which the strenuous efforts of the State should now be directed in a still larger measure than heretofore.

(iii) That primary education be extended in backward districts, especially in those inhabited mainly by aboriginal races, by the instrumentality of the Department pending the creation of school-boards, or by specially liberal grants-in-aid to those who are willing to set up and maintain schools.

2. *Legislation and Administration*: The Indian Education Commission recommended that the control of primary education should be made over to District and Municipal Boards.

3. *Encouragement of Indigenous Schools*: On this subject, the Commission was of the opinion that these schools deserved encouragement and incorporation in the official system of education.

4. *School Curriculum*:

(i) It should be adapted to the environment and should be simplified wherever possible.

(ii) Practical subjects, such as Indian methods of arithmetic and accounts should be introduced.

(iii) Managers should be free to choose the textbooks for their schools.

(iv) The utmost elasticity should be permitted regarding hours of the day and the season of the year during which the schools are to remain open.

(v) Instruction should be through the mother-tongue of the children.

5. *Finance*: The Commission recommended:

(i) A specific fund should be created for primary education.

(ii) The accounts of the primary education fund in municipal areas should be separated from those for the rural areas in order to avoid the expenditure in municipal areas of money meant for the villages.

(iii) The local funds should be utilised mainly for primary education and only incidentally – if at all – for secondary and collegiate education.

(iv) It was the duty of the Government to assist the local funds by a suitable system of grant-in-aid.

III. Recommendations on Secondary Education

1. *Openings of Model High School*: At least one model high school may be established in such districts, where they may be required in the interests of the people, and the people themselves may not be advanced or wealthy enough to establish such schools for themselves with a grant-in-aid.
2. *Bifurcation of the Secondary Education*: In the upper classes of high schools, there be two divisions; one leading to the Entrance examination of the Universities, the other of a more practical character, intended to fit youths for commercial or non-literary pursuits.

IV. Recommendation on Higher Education

The rate of aid to each college be determined by the strength of the staff, the expenditure on its maintenance, the efficiency of the institution and the wants of the locality.

V. Native Private Enterprise

The Commission observed, "Natives of India must constitute the most important of all agencies of education ... we think it well to put on record our unanimous opinion that withdrawal of direct departmental agency should not take place in favour of missionary bodies and the departmental institutions of the higher order should not be transferred to missionary management.

VI. Women Education

"... It will have been seen that female education is still in an extremely backward condition, and that it needs to be fostered in every legitimate way ... Hence we think it expedient to recommend "that public funds of all kinds—local, municipal and provincial—should be chargeable in an equitable proportion for the support of girls' schools as well as for boys' schools."

VII. Rules for Grant-in-Aid

The Commission made the following recommendations:

Grants-in-aid: (a) Institutions under private managers cannot be successful unless they are frankly accepted as an essential part of the general scheme of education. With a view to securing the cooperation of Government and non-Government institutions, the managers of the latter be consulted on matters of general educational interest, and that their students be admitted on equal terms to competition for certificates, scholarships and other public distinctions.

(b) In the conduct of all departmental examinations, managers of teachers of non-government schools should be associated as far as possible with the officers of the department.

(c) All scholarships and rewards that government confers should be given to pupils from all schools and not restricted to those in Government institutions only.

(d) The proximity of a government school should not be regarded as of itself a sufficient reason for refusing aid to a non-Government school.

(e) With the object of rendering assistance to schools in the form best suited to the circumstances of each province and thus to call forth the largest amount of local cooperation the grant-in-aid rules should be revised by the local Governments in consultation with the managers of schools. The revised rules should define without ambiguity the amount and duration of the aid to which an institution may be entitled and the conditions of grants for buildings, apparatus, and furniture.

(f) Every application for a grant-in-aid should receive an official reply and in case of refusal the reasons for such refusal should always be given.

(g) It should be a general principle that the grant-in-aid should depend (i) on locality, i.e., larger proportionate grants be given to schools in backward districts; and (ii) on the class of institution, i.e., grater proportionate aid be given to those in which a large amount of self-support cannot be expected, e.g., girls' schools and schools for lower castes and backward communities.

(h) Grants be paid without delay when they become due according to the rules.

(i) The revised rules for grant-in-aid and any subsequent alteration made in them should not be merely published in the official gazettes, but translated into the Indian languages, and communicated to the press, to the managers of aided and private institutions and to all who are likely to help in anyway in the spread of education.

(j) A periodically increasing provision should be made in the educational budget of each province for the expansion of aided institutions.

(k) Variety in the course of instruction in aided schools should be encouraged by grants for special subjects.

(l) Greater latitude should be given to the managers of aided schools in fixing the course of instruction and the medium through which it is conveyed.

(m) Care should be taken lest public examinations should become the means of practically imposing the same textbooks or curriculum on all schools.

(n) It should be distinctly laid down that Indians having the necessary qualifications should be employed as Inspectors of Schools more commonly than in the past.

VIII. Role of the Government and the Missionary Enterprise in Indian Education

The question how far the withdrawal of the State from the direct provision of means of higher education would throw such education into the hands of missionary bodies, held the foremost place in all the evidence bearing on the topic of withdrawal. Prominent officers of the department and many native gentlemen argue strongly against any withdrawal, on the ground that it must practically hand over higher education to missionaries. As a rule the missionary witnessed themselves, while generally advocating the policy of withdrawal, expressed quite the contrary opinion, stating that they neither expected nor desired that any power over education given up by the department should pass into their hands. In a country with such varied needs as India, we should deprecate any measure which would throw excessive influence over higher education into the hands of any single agency; and particularly into the hands of an agency which, however benevolent and earnest, cannot on all points be in sympathy with the mass of the community... At the same time we think it well to put on record our unanimous opinion that withdrawal of direct departmental agency should not take place in favour of missionary bodies and that departmental institutions of the higher order should not be transferred to missionary management ... In the point of view in which we are at present considering the question, missionary institutions hold an intermediate position between those managed by the department and those managed by the people for themselves. On the one hand, they are the outcome of private effort, but on the other they are not strictly local; nor will encouragement to them directly foster those habits of self-reliance and combination for purposes of public utility which is one of the objects of the grant-in-aid system to develop. Missionary institutions may serve the great purpose of showing what private effort can accomplish, and thus including other agencies to come forward. They should be allowed to follow their own independent course under the general supervision of the State; and so long as there is room and need for every variety of agency in the field of education, they should receive all the encouragement and aid that private effort can legitimately claim.

Subsequent Influence of the Report

Merits of the Report

1. It accepted the importance of primary education and gave detailed recommendations on the improvement of its various aspects.
2. It evolved a systematic system of grant-in-aid.
3. It provided encouragement to indigenous system of education.
4. It gave encouragement to private initiative.
5. It laid down the policy regarding the role of missionaries.
6. It recommended diversification of courses at the secondary stage.
7. It attached importance to the spread of women education.

Limitations and Shortcomings of the Report

1. It was not a wise policy on the part of the government to withdraw gradually from the secondary education sector.
2. Primary education was entrusted to organisations and institutions which were not reasonably financially sound.
3. Recommendations on religious education were not realistic.
4. There was very high expectations from the Education Departments.
5. Grant-in-aid rules on the 'basis of results' was not a healthy practice.
6. Expansion of higher education resulted in dilution of standards.

EVALUATION OF RECOMMENDATIONS: POSITIVE AND NEGATIVE EFFECTS

Neglect of Financial Aspect: "The financial resources of the Boards were going to be extremely slender and to expect them to do justice to their charge was to expect the impossible. But the Commission failed to see this. If the Government had not tried to evade their responsibilities, then there would have been a fair chance of achieving some good results : but that was not to be. The Government shifted their responsibilities to the newly formed Boards and left them to experiment with such a vital subject as the education of the people". (*A.N. Basu: Education in Modern India*)

Reiteration of Most of the Recommendations of Wood's Despatch: "This disregard of the financial implication of the problem robs the recommendations of the Indian Education Commission of a large part of their utility". (*Nurullah and Naik: A History of Education in India,* p. 350)

"The net result achieved by the Commission was not to commensurate with the volume of its Report. It practically reiterated the principles which had already been accepted years ago in Wood's Despatch. It only elaborated some of the points and added some emphasis here and there". (*A.N. Basu*)

Defective Secondary Education: "Secondary Education succeeded in producing literary minded persons and failed to turn out the practically minded workers best suited for the battle of life." (*A.N. Basu*)

Lack of Appropriate Measures: "Although their hopes upon the system of instruction becoming more thorough and more scientific, they had no measures to recommend whereby it could be made so." (*Report of the Calcutta University Commission, Vol. I*)

Comparative Neglect of the Comprehensive Survey of Higher Education: The Government's Resolution appointing the Commission had stated, that it would not be necessary for the Commission to enquire into the general working of the Indian

Universities, which are controlled by corporations comprising representation of all classes interested in collegiate education". The Commission was also not to go into the functioning of professional colleges. Thus the Commission did not study the problems of higher education in a comprehensive manner.

Educational Awakening: "The historical value of this document (Report) is incalculable. The enquiry of the Commission led to great educational awakening in India and its main findings dominated Indian educational policy till 1902". (*Nurullah and Naik : A History of Education in India,* pp. 26-27)

3

Lord Curzon's Educational Policy and National Education Movement

ARROGANCE OF LORD CURZON : CURZON–THE VICEROY MOST HATED BY THE INDIANS

In spite of the fact that he took several measures to bring about reforms in different areas, Lord Curzon remained the most hated Viceroy that came to India. His sarcastic remarks about Indians greatly offended the Indians. Here we give a very brief but typical example of his arrogance. "I hope I am making no false or arrogant claim when I say that the highest ideal of truth is to a large extent a Western concept ...Asiatics deliberately deviate from the truth".

During the tenure of Lord Curzon, India witnessed tremendous national awakening in the wake of the 'Partition of Bengal' in 1905.

Lord Curzon's policy gave birth to militant nationalism in India. The trio of Bal-Lal-Pal, i.e., Bal Gangadhar Tilak, Lala Lajpat Rai and Bipin Chandra Pal led the freedom struggle and brought about national awakening among the masses.

CHIEF EDUCATIONAL EVENTS DURING CURZON'S PERIOD

1. Educational Conference (1901)
2. Government Resolution on Educational Policy (1904)
3. Indian Universities Commission (1902)

4. Indian Universities Act (1904)
5. National Education Movement (1905) (*Discussed in the next chapter*)

EDUCATIONAL CONFERENCE (1901)

During the viceroyalty of Lord Curzon, education in India was reviewed very critically and steps were taken to improve the various branches of education. In 1901, Lord Curzon convened at Simla an educational conference which was attended by a few selected educationists and the Provincial Directors of Public Instruction. This was the first conference on all-India basis. The conference continued for a fortnight and passed 150 resolutions. Lord Curzon took a prominent part in drafting the resolutions which formed the basis of the Government of India's Resolution on Educational Policy (1904).

INDIAN UNIVERSITIES COMMISSION (1902)

Circumstances Leading to the Appointment of the Indian Universities Commission (1902)

There were three important reasons for the appointment of the Commission. First, the defects of the university education were very glaring and nothing had been done to remodel the Indian Universities since they were established and the matter was left untouched by the Indian Education Commission of 1882. Secondly, the London University, which had served as a model to Indian Universities was reorganised in 1898. Hence it was considered worthwhile to go into the various aspects of university education in India. Third, the conference of educationalists in 1901 had made several recommendations. On January 27, 1902 the Indian University Commission was appointed and it reported in June of the same year.

Terms of Reference

To enquire into the conditions and prospects of the universities established in British India, to consider and report upon any proposals which have been or may be made for improving their constitution and working and to recommend to the Governor General-in-Council such measures as may tend to elevate the standard of university teaching to promote the advancement of learning.

Major Recommendations of the Indian Universities Commission (1902)

1. *Adoption of the Model of the University of London*: This model of the London University as modified in 1898 had the following features:

(i) Every university ought to be a teaching university.
(ii) No college should be allowed full privileges unless it was thoroughly well-staffed.
(iii) Teachers must always be intimately associated with the government of the University.
(iv) The supreme governing body of the university was its Senate which should not be too large.

2. *Reorganisation of Senate and Syndicate*: The members of the Senate should be reduced and their terms should be five years. The number of the members of the syndicate should be between nine and fifteen.

3. *Teaching Facilities*: After amending the constitution of the universities, certain facilities for teaching should be given to them.

4. *Proper Representation of Teachers*: There should be a proper representation of the teachers and the scholars of the affiliated colleges in the University Senate.

5. *Rules for Recognition of Colleges*: There should be proper arrangement for teaching in the colleges affiliated to the universities, and the rules for recognition should be strictly observed and enforced.

6. *Supervision of Colleges*: Affiliated colleges should be strictly supervised by the universities.

7. *Appointment of Teachers*: Universities should appoint

teachers to impart higher education.

8. *Curriculum Reforms*: Certain proper amendments should be made in the curriculum and the examination system of the universities.

9. *Hostel Facilities*: Hostels should be built for the students.

10. *Scholarships*: According to the position of the students, the arrangement for scholarships should take place.

11. *Three Years Degree Course*: The standard of the Matric examination should be high and while abolishing the inter examination, the curriculum of B.A. should be of three years.

12. *College Managing Committees*: A Managing Committee should be there for every college which, besides managing the college concerned, should also appoint competent teachers and pay attention towards the discipline of the students and the construction of buildings and hostels, etc.

Evaluation of the Report

Since the Commission was precluded from discussing secondary education, it could not deal with the problem in its entirety.

Secondly, the Commission did not discuss the fundamental problems of university organisation.

The Commission's recommendations on University Education have been regarded as rehabilitation and strengthening of the existing system.

INDIAN UNIVERSITIES ACT (1904)

Background of the Act

Lord Curzon accorded the top priority in his programme of educational reforms to university education reform. It was to help him in this task that he appointed the Indian Universities Commission (1902) to enquire into the conditions of universities, to consider and report upon proposals for improving their constitution and working. After the submission of the report, the Indian Universities Act was passed on March 21, 1904 in the Imperial Legislative Council in the face of bitter opposition especially from G.K. Gokhale. The Act, by and large, embodied the main recommendations of the Commission. It also included the main suggestions of the Government of India's Resolution on Indian Educational Policy.

Main Provisions

1. *Enlargement of Functions of Universities*: Universities were given the right of teaching along with the right of conducting examinations. In short, their scope was enlarged. Universities had the right to appoint teachers to conduct teaching and they inspired them to carry on research, to manage libraries and laboratories and to make out plans to bring about discipline among the students.

2. *Reforms in the Senate*: Upto the moment the number of the seats in the Senate of the universities were not fixed and the Government used to make life-long nominations. According to this Act, the number was fixed. The minimum number was fifty and the maximum number was hundred. Their term was determined for five years.

3. *Elected Members of the Syndicate*: According to the Indian Universities Act, the members of the Senate got the right to elect members. Such elected members, were not to be more than twenty for the universities of Calcutta, Bombay and Madras and fifteen for other universities.

4. *Legal Status of Syndicate*: Legal status was given to the syndicates of the universities.

5. *Representation of Teachers*: In these syndicates proper representation of professors was made compulsory.

6. *Powers of the Government*: The Government secured the right to make amendments and reforms and give approval to the rules framed by the Senates of the university. The

Government also had the right to make laws in this regard by themselves.

7. *Strict Rules for Recognition of Colleges*: Rules in regard to granting of recognition were made strict. In order to raise the standards of education, the syndicate could cause the inspection of the colleges imparting higher education.

8. *Fixing the Territorial Jurisdiction of the Universities*: To this day, the territorial jurisdiction of universities was not fixed, with the result that in some places some colleges had secured recognition from two universities. But now, in the 27th Article of this Act, it was made clear that the Governor General shall by his ordinary or extraordinary orders, fix the territorial jurisdiction of the universities and according to this provision the relations between the university and the colleges shall be established and maintained.

9. *Recognition of Schools*: In addition to the recognition of schools by the Department of Public Instruction (Education), secondary schools had to obtain recognition from a university if they desired to present pupils at the Matriculation examination conducted by the university. Regulations were framed by the universities for the recognition of schools for this purpose. Similarly rules were framed with a view to minimising the conflict between the Department and the University.

GOVERNMENT RESOLUTION ON EDUCATION POLICY (1904)

Introduction: In pursuance of the conference of the educationists at Simla in 1901 and with a view to give a clear cut direction to Government's activities as well to the private the Government passed a Resolution in 1904.

Extracts from the Resolution

Primary Education: The active expansion of primary education is one of the most active duties of the State.

Secondary Education: Whether these schools are managed by

public authority or by private persons, and whether they receive aid from public funds or not, the Government is bound in the interests of the community to see that the education provided in them is sound. It must, for example, satisfy itself in each case that a secondary school is actually wanted, that its financial stability is assured, that its managing body, where there is one, is properly constituted; that it teaches the proper subject upto a proper standard; that due provision has been made for the instruction, health, recreation, and discipline of the pupils; that the teachers are suitable as regards character, number and qualifications; and that the fees to be paid will not involve such competition with any existing schools as will be unfair and injurious to the interests of education. Such are the conditions upon which alone schools should be eligible to receive grant-in-aid or to send up pupils to compete for, or receive pupils in enjoyment of Government scholarships and schools complying with them will be ranked as 'recognised schools'.

Religious Education: In Government institutions the instruction is, and must continue to be, exclusively secular.

The Resolution also detailed the state of education in India. Important facts are summarised here.

Educational Facilities: (1) Twenty percent villages in India had a school; (2) Twenty five boys received education at school; (3) Less than 3 percent of girls went to school.

Main Characteristics of the System of Education: (1) Getting government service was the aim of education; (2) Education system was examination-dominated; (3) By and large courses were bookish and theorical; (4) Methods of instruction encouraged memorisation and not developing intellect; (5) English was encouraged at the cost of vernacular languages; (6) Technical education was neglected.

Evaluation of the Resolution: In the words of A.N. Basu, "Though the diagnose was correct, the remedy suggested was neither appropriate nor opportune".

MEASURES FOR THE IMPROVEMENT OF EDUCATION

A. Measures Taken by Lord Curzon to Improve Secondary Schools

1. Rules of recognition of schools were made quite strict.
2. Grant-in-aid to private schools was raised.
3. Large financial grants were sanctioned to provincial governments for the salaries of the staff, equipment, buildings and hostels, etc.
4. Training of secondary teachers was stressed.
5. Modifications were made in the curricula.
6. Mother-tongue was made compulsory as the medium of instruction at the middle stage. English was also to be learnt for facilitating progress at the high school stage where English was the medium of instruction.
7. The inspectorate was strengthened. Salaries were increased and steps were taken to make them efficient.

B. Measures for the Qualitative Improvement of Primary Education

In high education, Lord Curzon laid more emphasis on the quality of education as against quantity. However, at the primary stage both aspects, i.e., quality and quantity were emphasised. Large non-recurring grants to primary education were sanctioned.

For the qualitative improvement of primary education, Lord Curzon took the following measures:

One. Training of primary teachers was stressed; *Two*. Curricula was revised; *Three*. System of 'Payment by Results' was abandoned.

C. Reforms in Higher Education

Important measures were:

1. Appointment of the Indian Universities Commission (1902),
2. Government Resolution (1904),
3. Indian Universities Act (1904)

CRITICAL EVALUATION OF LORD CURZON'S CONTRIBUTION TO EDUCATION

At the outset it must be admitted that on account of his arrogance, hatred for Indian intelligentsia, condemnation of moral standards of the Indians, tall claim of truthful nature of the Europeans, sectarian politics, and partition of Bengal, Lord Curzon became the most hated Viceroy that ever came to India. Accordingly, his every action was considered as anti-India, irrespective of the merits.

Observations made by Nurullah and Naik regarding Curzon's contribution to education are quite appropriate. These depict the true picture. "We are now in a position to estimate Curzon's contribution to Indian education. In his own time, Curzon came in for every bitter criticism for reasons already explained. But fortunately, we are no longer blinded by the controversies of the period. With her characteristic catholicity of heart, India has forgiven the insults which Curzon directed at her patriotic children, just as she forgave the vilification of Charles Grant or Macaulay and now that we can see the scene more clearly it is possible to evaluate Curzon's work in an objective and critical manner." The authors further observed, "In fact the tide was already turned and the commonest sentiment towards him in educational circles today is of appreciation and understanding : Curzon, it is now admitted, did yeoman service to the cause of education." According to them "Curzon was the author of the great movement for educational reconstruction which started in the beginning of the century."

Nurullah and Naik list the following specific contribution of Lord Curzon to Indian education:

1. He laid the foundation of the reform of Indian universities which gathered momentum in later years.
2. In primary education he started a new drive for expansion.

3. Agricultural education received a tremendous impetus at the hands of Curzon. He laid down that every important province must have its own agriculture college.
4. Curzon was the founder of department of Archaeology in India.
5. He started the movement for Central's responsibility in educational finance.
6. He created the Education Department in the Government of India.
7. He encouraged the study of the modern Indian languages.
8. He instituted scholarships for sending Indian students for technological studies abroad.
9. He encouraged Schools of Art.

Nurullah and Naik sum up Lord Curzon's contribution to education in these words, "In short, it may be said of Curzon that he touched almost every aspect of Indian education and touched nothing that he did not reform."

Prof. A.N. Basu's assessment of Curzon's work in education is as, " ... though the diagnose was correct, the remedy suggested was neither appropriate nor opportune. Lord Curzon was right in many of the things he said; but it was the way in which he wanted to reform that raised gave suspicious in the minds of educated Indians. They thought that this reform move camouflaged some deep political motive."

Prof. Amarnath Jha pays his tribute to Lord Curzon in these words, "Now that the ashes of the numerous strifes are cold, all Indians are grateful to the wise statesmanship of the great Viceroy who did so much to preserve our ancient monuments and raise our educational standards. By these achievements he still lives, and generations of Indian will bless him for there."

4

Growth of National Consciousness

National Education Movement

INTRODUCTION

The beginning of the growth of national consciousness may be traced to the various revolts that took place against the atrocities of the British officials in different parts of India and culminated in the First War of Indian Independence 1857. The birth of the Indian National Congress in 1885 provided a new direction to national consciousness. The Partition of Bengal in 1905 by Lord Curzon gave great impetus to the growth of national consciousness which spread to different areas all over India. With the growth of national consciousness, National Education Movement emerged.

PHASES OF NATIONAL EDUCATION MOVEMENT

Broadly speaking, we may divide the National Education Movement in the following phases:

1. Phase one : (1890 to 1904)
2. Phase two : Around 1905 (Partition of Bengal – Lord Curzon's time)
3. Phase three : 1921-22 (Non-Cooperation Movement)
4. Phase four : 1937-39 (Wardha Scheme of Education and Formation of Congress Ministries). This phases has been taken up separately.

First Phase: National Education Movement

Gooroo Das Banerjee, the first Indian Vice-Chancellor, foreshadowed in broadlines "the entire pedagogic pattern of the National Council of Education" in the course of the Convocation Addresses (1890-1892) and suggested among others, the urgency of the introduction of the mother tongue as the medium of instruction. About the same time Rabindranath Tagore in his paper on *Shikshar Hereter* published in Dec.-Jan., 1892-93 in *Sadhana* pointed out in a clear manner the inadequacy of the prevailing system of education under the British rule and pleaded for the acceptance of Bengali as the medium of instruction.

Satish Chandra Mukherjee, the Editor of the *Dawn* (1897-1913) observed in 1898 how the prevalent system of university education had failed to satisfy everyone of the parties concerned: "From the point of view of savants, he observed, "it is regarded as a failure since as an examining and not a teaching university, the Indian university has hardly succeeded in drawing to itself a body of learned men who devoted their time and energies wholly to the cause of original research in every department of learning. Nor from the political or the Government point of view, is the university the success which the founder expected it should be ... from the commercial point of view, it is looked upon with disfavour by the majority of graduates who with a smattering of literary or semi-scientific instruction find it hard even to earn a bare pittance to keep body and soul together."

Dawn Society located in a room at Vidyasagar College, then called the Metropolitan Institution was founded in 1902 by Prof. Haridas Mukherjee with the objective of conceiving it as an instrument of a moral and intellectual revolution among the youth of Bengal so as to prepare them ultimately for political revolution to achieve the freedom of the country ... The young men that were trained in this institution were the pioneers of the National Education Movement which was organised by the Foundation of the National Council of Education and the Bengal National College as its central institution, with Sri Aurobindo as its first Principal and Satish Chandra Mukherjee as its first Executive Head or Superintendent. "It was like the Encyclopaedists passing the way of the French Revolution" to quote Dr. Radha Kumud Mukerjee. The programme of training of the Dawn Society comprised regulated reading of select literature in its library and weekly lectures.

[(Prof.) Haridas Mukherjee and (Prof.) Uma Mukherjee, *The Origins of the National Education Movement* (1905-1910), Jadavpur University, Calcutta, 1957]

Second Phase : Intensification of National Education Movement During Lord Curzon's Period and Partition of Bengal (1905)

Political developments during Viceroyalty of Lord Curzon gave great impetus to the National Education Movement. His utterances of insults of the Indians and Partition of Bengal created intense hatred for him. Political controversies generated by him were invariably carried into educational field. To quote Nurullah and Naik "...officials and non-officials fought over questions of primary or higher education in more or less the same way in which they came into conflict over political issues". Even the good measures of Curzon were misunderstood and therefore attacked by his contemporaries who regarded Curzon as a thorough 'imperialist' and a 'bully'. They were convinced that Curzon's primary objective was to strengthen British empire in India and for this he was using education also as an instrument. His actions resulted in the rise of militant nationalism. The partition of Bengal provided the necessary fuel to the nationalist agony.

Apart from the Partition of Bengal, there were several educational differences in the approach of Lord Curzon and Indian leaders. These issues were:

First. Indian leaders were of the view that expansion of educational facilities for the masses should be prepared for qualitative improvement.

Second. Lord Curzon wanted more government control and interference in the functioning of educational institutions for their improvement. The leaders felt that this policy was intended to Sabotage the development of national feeling in the minds of educated Indians.

Third. Lord Curzon laid more emphasis on primary education whereas the Indian leaders did not want to neglect secondary and higher education.

Four. The leaders wanted complete and speedy Indianisation of the Education Department.

Five. There was a strong feeling that Curzon's educational policy was intended to develop a sense of loyalty to British rule and not to mother-India.

Six. Climax came with the Partition of Bengal and its '*Swadeshi*' Movement, i.e., '*Swadeshi*' goods, '*Swadesh*' educational institutions.

Setting up of National Education Institutions

The partition of Bengal in 1905 was "the signal for an agitation such as India had not hitherto-witnessed. Students of the Rangpur Zila School and Technical School were persecuted for organising public meetings. A public conference held on November 7, 1905 resolved on taking the education of the Rangpur students into their own hands and started the Rangpur National School on November 8, 1905 "with the object of imparting education—both general and technical." A twenty-men Executive Committee was constituted. As reported in the 'Calendar of the National Council of Education' for 1906-1908, many of the members of the Executive Committee subscribed Rs.100 each month for the support of the National School and donations amounting to Rs.10,000 wee raised from local and other sources. The school started with about 300 boys on its rolls.

The Bengal National College was formally inaugurated on August 14, 1906.

National Council of Education

The National Council of Education was registered on June 1, 1906 under the Act XXI of 1860.

The scheme of studies included Primary Stage (extending over three years); Secondary Stage-Lower (extending over five years); Secondary Stage-Upper (extending over two years) and the Collegiate Stage (extending over four years).

The movement for the National Education was not confined to Bengal alone. It spread to other parts of India also.

Object of the Council and Chief Characteristics of Education

The object of the council is to impart education—literary as well as scientific and technical—on national lines and exclusively under national control, not in opposition to, but standing apart from the existing systems of primary, secondary and university education.

Education on national lines should imply among other things:

(a) Imparting of education, ordinarily through the medium of the vernaculars, English being a compulsory subject.

(b) 1. The preparation of suitable textbooks, especially in the vernaculars.

2. Promoting of physical and moral education and providing for denominational religious education out of funds specifically contributed for that purpose and inspiring students with a genuine love for, and a real desire to serve their country.

Such religious education is not to include the enforcement of religious rites and practices.

3. Attaching a special importance to a knowledge of the country, or literature, history and philosophy and incorporating with the best oriental ideals of life and thought and the best assimilable ideals of the West.
4. Imparting of scientific, professional and technical education chiefly in those branches of science, arts and industries which are best calculated to develop the material resources of the country, and to satisfy its pressing wants.
5. Inclusion in scientific education generally of a knowledge of the scientific truths embodied in oriental learning and in medical education specially of such scientific truths as are to be found in the Ayurvedic and Hakimi systems.
6. (a) Exacting of a high standard of proficiency, and

   (b) Enforcement of strict discipline including paying proper regard to the religious sentiments and customs of the different sections of the community in accordance with the best traditions of the country.

Third Phase : National Education Movement (1920-22)

Introduction

In an earlier chapter reference has been made to the National Council of Education (1906). The tempo created by the partition died out, particularly after the reunion of Bengal. The second upheaval occurred in 1920-22. The martial law atrocities in the Punjab and the inadequacy of the Montford Reforms (1919) fanned the flame of national feelings in the country. Just at this juncture, Mahatma Gandhi appeared on the scene and he launched the '*Non-cooperation Movement*'. The Resolution passed at the Nagpur Congress in 1920 advised the "gradual withdrawal of children from schools and colleges owned, aided or controlled by Government, and in place of such schools and colleges, the establishment of national schools and colleges in the various provinces."

Main Features of the National Education Movement

National education movement emphasised three points: (1) Indian control of education, (2) teaching the love of motherland, and (3) no servile imitation of the West.

MRS. ANNIE BESANT ON NATIONAL EDUCATION

1. National education must live in an atmosphere of proud and glorious patriotism, and this atmosphere must be kept sweet, fresh, and bracing by the study of Indian literature, Indian history, Indian triumphs in science, in art, in politics, in war, in colonization, in manufactures, in trade, in commerce.

2. National education must meet the national temperament at every point, and develop the national character. India is not to become a lesser – nor even a greater – England, but to evolve into a mightier India.

3. British ideals are good for Britain, but it is India's ideals that are good for India. We do not want echoes nor monotones; we want a choral melody of nations, mirroring colour, and trees, and flowers, and mountains, and sky wear but a single hue? Harmonious variety and not monotony is the mark of perfection. Away from all apologies for India, with all deprecatory explanations of India's ways and customs, and traditions.

4. India is herself, and needs not to be justified; for verily, God has evolved no greater, no more exquisite nationality than India's among all the broken reflections of His own perfect beauty.

5. National education must be controlled by Indians, shaped by Indians, carried on by Indians. It must hold up Indian ideals of devotion, wisdom and morality, and must be permeated by

the Indian religious spirit rather than fed on the platter of the creeds. The spirit is spacious, tolerant, all-embracing, and recognises that man goes to God along many roads and that all the prophets came from Him.

SPREAD OF NATIONAL EDUCATION MOVEMENT

Dr. Pattabhi Sitaramaya, a former congress President has described the spread of the movement in the monumental publication "*History of the Indian National Congress*" in these words,

"National universities, national colleges and national schools of all grades were started in different parts of the country. The student movement in the U.P., the Punjab and the Bombay Presidency was in full swing. Bengal was not behind and, and Calcutta witnessed one of those thrilling scenes which were not few or far between in the course of that memorable year and a half. About the middle of January, on an appeal by Deshbandhu C.R. Das, thousands of students left their colleges and examinations. Gandhi visited Calcutta and opened the National College on the 4th of February. He also visited Patna for a second time and formally opened the national College and inaugurated the Bihar Vidyapeeth. Thus, in the course of less than four months, the National Muslim University of Aligarh, the Gujarat Vidyapeeth, the Bihar Vidyapeeth, the Kashi Vidyapeeth, the Bengal National University, the Tilak Maharashtra Vidyapeeth and a large number of national schools of all grades, with thousands of students on the rolls, were started in all parts of the country as a result of the great impetus given to national education".

SAD END OF THE MOVEMENT

Nurullah and Naik in this regard observe,

"Unfortunately, a set-back to the whole movement came in too early. The tempo of the Non-cooperation Movement cooled down after some time, and as some cases of violence began to occur, Gandhiji withdrew the Movement altogether. The fundamental concepts of Swaraj within one year did not materialise and as the prospect of Independence receded into the background, the enthusiasm of the students naturally began to wane. The national leaders also realised that it would be wrong to expect the students to sacrifice the whole of their career. The earlier policy of non-cooperation was accordingly changed and, excepting a few top-ranking institutions, others were allowed to seek government recognition again and the students were also permitted, unless they desired to devote their whole life to the national cause, to seek admission to recognised schools and complete their training. By 1922, the tide had almost ebbed.

This second upheaval in national education, as the above account will show, differed materially from the first in several respects. It was more intensive, and more widespread; the numbers of students and teachers involved in it were far larger; it contributed more largely to constructive educational thought; and the movement continued to exist and no useful pioneer work even after non-cooperation came to an end, while the first upheaval hardly left any such mileposts behind".

NATIONAL UNIVERSITIES

Gurukul University, Kangri, Haridwar: This institution founded as a small elementary school before the first National Education Movement (1905). Although a national education system had been initiated by Swami Dayanand much earlier by Arya Pratinidhi Sabha Punjab in 1902 grew into a university in due course. It declined to seek government grant as it wanted to have an honourable independence, free from any government control, for achieving its noble and national objectives. In 1924, it was shifted to Kangri so that it could work in 'sylvan solitude' away from the 'uneducational influences of city life'. Students were admitted between the ages 6 and 8, and they pursued studies for 14 years to become a '*Snatak*' or graduate. The Gurukul Branch for girls is located at Dehradun. (Gurukul means the 'home of thc teacher') Chief features of the institution were: (1) Residential institution; (2) Free education along with free lodging and boarding; (3) Equality of treatment; (4) Developing qualities of endurance and hardship; (5) Emphasis on *Brahmacharya* and character building; (6) Stress on vedic studies. The University is popularly known as Gurukul Kangri.

Kashi Vidyapeeth: An institution of national importance was established in 1921 in Banaras, due to the efforts of Mahatma Gandhi, Dr. Bhagwan Dass, and others as they wanted to introduce national education suiting to Indian needs, aspirations and culture. It has grown into national importance and provides education upto the post-graduate classes and has research facilities. Lal Bahadur Shastri, the late Prime Minister of India, was a graduate of this institution. Eminent scholars like Dr. Bhagwan Dass, Acharya Narendra Deva, Acharya Kripalani, Dr. Sampurnanand, and Shri Prakasha had been on the staff of this institution.

Jamia Millia Islamia: One of the national universities of All-India character was founded in 1920 at Aligarh. Its necessity was urged by such leaders as Mahatma Gandhi, Maulana Muhammad Ali, Hakim Ajmal Khan, Dr. M.A. Ansari and Dr. Zakir Hussain. It shifted to Delhi in 1925. At that time it refused to seek recognition or grants at the hands of the British Government, a s it preferred 'the hardships and ordeals of an honourable independence' for achieving its noble ambitions. Its objectives were to broaden the education of the youth on their own cultural heritage, to inculcate the spirit of service, tolerance, self-control and self-respect, to provide opportunities of self-expression, to develop initiative and responsibility and to build character. Dr. Zakir Hussain, the distinguished educationist, who became the President of India in 1967, was the Vice-Chancellor of Jamia Millia for 22 years from 1926-1948.

Visva-Bharati: Visva-Bharati was established on May 6, 1922 by Gurudev Rabindranath Tagore, with his endowment. Its objectives were:

1. To bring the diverse cultures of the East into more intimate relationship with one another.
2. To develop concord between the East and the West.
3. To develop feeling of international harmony and brotherhood.

5

Gokhale's Bill, Government Resolution on Education and Sadler Commission (1917-1919)

GOKHALE'S EFFORTS AND BILL FOR COMPULSORY PRIMARY EDUCATION (1910-12)

Introduction

Gokhale as Champion of Compulsory Education: Gopal Krishan Gokhale (1866-1915) besides being a statesman, social reformer and educator, was a great champion of compulsory primary education in India. He was a Professor and Principal of Poona Ferguson College for a number of years, President of the Indian National Congress (1905), founder of the Servants of India Society and Member of Imperial Legislature. Between 1910 and 1913 Gokhale made heroic efforts to make the government accept the principle of compulsory education. The demand for compulsory education was strengthened by the fact that the Gaekwar of Baroda had introduced compulsory education throughout his State in 1906. Gokhale moved the resolution for compulsory education in 1910 in the Imperial Council .

EXTRACTS FROM GOKHALE'S RESOLUTION, 1910

I beg to place the following resolution before the Council for its consideration:

"That this Council recommends that a beginning should be

made in the direction of making elementary education free and compulsory throughout the country, and that a mixed Commission of officials and non-officials be appointed at an early date to frame definite proposals."

Extracts from the Speech

My Lord, there is much truth in the homely adage that where there is a will there is a way. I think that this question of compulsory and free primary education is now in this country the question of questions. The well-being of millions upon millions of children who are waiting to be brought under the humanizing influence of education depends upon it. The increased efficiency of the individual, the higher general level of intelligence, the stiffening of the moral backbone of large sections of the community, none of these things can come without such education. In fact, the whole of our future as a nation is inextricably bound up with it. My Lord, however this resolution may be disposed of here today. I feel that in this matter we are bound to win.

Important Suggestions Contained in the Resolution

Important suggestions contained in his resolution, moved in the Legislative Council, were as follows:

1. That in the area where 35% boys were receiving education, elementary education should be made free and compulsory. This provision should apply to the age group of 6 to 10 years.
2. The cost of primary education should be shared by the Provincial Government and Local Bodies. The Local Bodies and the Government Bodies should bear the expenditure in the ratio of 1:2.
3. A secretary should be appointed to organise, supervise and look after the primary education.

4. There should be a separate Department in the Central Government to draw up scheme for the expansion of primary education; and in the budget statement there should be a portion describing the progress of primary education.

On the assurance of the Government of India, that the whole question should be examined, Gokhale withdrew the Bill.

GOKHALE'S SECOND ATTEMPT (MARCH 18, 1912)

On March 16, 1911, Gokhale brought in a bill to make better provision in the extension of compulsory education. On March 18, he moved the Resolution that his Bill be examined by a Select Committee of 15 members of the Viceroy's Council.

Main suggestions contained in the Bill are given below:

(a) He suggested that compulsory primary education should be introduced in the areas where a certain percentage was fixed by the Governor-General in Council.

(b) After securing the sanction of Government, the local body shall enforce the rule. Local Bodies at their end were to have the right to introduce compulsion in the whole or part of the area under their jurisdiction.

(c) Local bodies were also given the right to levy cess to meet the cost of free and compulsory primary education.

(d) Expenditure on education was to be spared by the Local Bodies and the Provincial Government in the ratio of 1:2.

(e) It was also suggested by Gokhale that primary education should be made compulsory for the boys of the age group of 6 to 10, and the defaulting guardians should be penalised for non-compliance of the provisions of sending their wards to recognised primary schools.

(f) It was also recommended that the primary education shall also be made compulsory for girls.

(g) Guardians whose monthly income is less than Rs.10/- should not be asked to pay any fee.

Extracts of Gokhale's Elementary Education Bill, 1911

This, my Lord, is briefly the whole of my Bill. It is a small and humble attempt to suggest the first steps of a journey, which is bound to prove long and tedious, but which must be performed, if the mass of our people are to emerge from their present conditions. My Lord, this question of a universal diffusion of education in India depends, almost more than any other questions, on the hearty and sympathetic cooperation of the government and the leaders of the people. The government must, in the first instance, adopt definitely the policy of such diffusion as its own, and it must, secondly, not grudge to find the bulk of the money, which will be required for it, as governments in most other civilised countries are doing. And this is what we are entitled to ask at the hands of the government in the name of justice, for the honour of the government itself, and in the highest interests of popular well-being. The leaders of the people, on their side, must bring to this task high enthusiasm, which will not be chilled by difficulties, courage, which will not shrink from encountering unpopularity it need be, and readiness to make sacrifices, whether of money or time or energy, which the cause may require.

If a beginning is made without further delay, if both the government and the people persevere with the task in the right spirit, the whole problem may be solved before another generation rises to take our place. If this happens the next generation will enter upon its own security of success. As for us, it will be enough to have laboured for such an end— laboured with not only profound humility but also profound wisdom in the faith which says:

"I do not ask to see the distant scene;

One step enough for me."

Extracts from Gokhale's Speech in 1912 in the Council

My Lord, I know that my Bill will be thrown out before the day closes, I make no complaint, I shall not even feel depressed. I know too well the story of the preliminary efforts that were required even in England, before the Act of 1870 was passed. Moreover, I have always felt and have often said that we, of the present generation in India, can only hope to serve our country by our failures. The men and women who will be privileged to serve her by their successes will come later. We must be content to accept cheerfully the place that has been allotted to us in our onward march. The Bill thrown out today, will come back again and again, till on the stepping-stones of its dead selves, a measure will ultimately rise which will spread the light of knowledge throughout the land. It may be that this anticipation will not come true. It may be that our efforts may not conduce even indirectly to the promotion of the great cause which we all have at heart and that they may turn out after all to be nothing better than the mere ploughing of the sands of the seashore. But, my Lord, whatever fate awaits our labours, one thing is clear. We shall be entitled to feel that we have done our duty, and, where the call of duty is clear, it is better even to labour and fail than not to labour at all. *Rejection of the Bill*: The Bill was rejected by 38 votes to 13.

IMPACT OF THE BILL

Gokhale's efforts bore fruit gradually. His work was taken up by Vithalbhai Patel. In 1917, he moved in the Bombay Legislative Council, a Bill for the introduction of compulsory/primary education in the Municipal limits of Bombay. The Bill was passed with some modifications and became the first Law on compulsory education in India. It is known as the Patel Act of 1918.

GOVERNMENT RESOLUTION ON EDUCATION POLICY (1913)

Introduction

While rejecting Gokhale's Bill, the Government promised to extend recurring and non-recurring grants to primary education. The Government could not entirely ignore the growing popular demand for the spread of mass education. The seeds sown by Gokhale came up quickly for harvest. Gokhale's Bill created a flutter in the British Parliament also. In the course of the discussion on the Indian budget, the Under-Secretary of State for India admitted the need for paying more attention to Indian education. As a result, the Government of India passed the Resolution on Educational Policy on February 21, 1913.

Extracts from the Government Resolution on Educational Policy (1913)

The proposition that illiteracy must be broken down and that primary education has, in the present circumstances of India, a predominant claim upon the public funds, represents accepted policy no longer open to discussion. For financial and administrative reasons of decisive weight the Government of India have refused to recognise principle of compulsory education; but they desire the widest possible extension of primary education on a voluntary basis. As regards free elementary education, the time has not yet arrived when it is practicable to dispense wholly with fees without injustice to the many villages which are waiting for the provision of schools. The fees derived from those pupils who can pay them are now devoted to the maintenance and expansion of primary education, and a total remission of fees would involve to a certain extent a more prolonged postponement of a provision of schools in villages without them. In some provinces elementary education is already free and in the majority of provinces liberal provision is already made for giving free elementary instruction to those boys whose parents cannot afford to pay fees. Local Governments have been requested to extend the application of the principle of free elementary education amongst the poorer and more backward sections of the population. Further than this, it is not possible at present to go...

It is the desire and hope of the Government of India to see in the not distant future some 91,000 primary public schools added to the 100,000 which already exist for boys and to double the 4½ millions of the pupils who now receive instruction, in them.

Major Provisions of the Resolution

(i) There should be sufficient expansion of lower primary schools, where along with instruction in the three R's, children should be taught drawing, knowledge of the village map, nature study and physical exercises.

(ii) Simultaneously, upper primary schools should be opened at the proper places and if need be, the lower primary schools should be raised to the status of upper primary schools.

(iii) Local Boards' schools should be established in place of private-aided schools.

(iv) Maktabs and Pathshalas should be adequately subsidised.

(v) The inspection and management of private schools should be made more efficient.

(vi) In most of the parts of India, it may not be practicable to prescribe separate curricula for rural and urban, but in the urban schools there is sufficient scope for teaching Geography and organising school excursions etc.

(vii) The teachers should have passed vernacular middle examination and received one year's training.

(viii) Provision be made for refresher courses for the teachers of primary education during vacations.

(ix) A trained teacher should get a salary not less than Rs.12 p.m. Again there should be provision for his increment in salary, pension and provident fund.

(x) The number of students under one teacher should generally range between 30 and 40.

(xi) Improvement should be made in the condition of middle and secondary vernacular schools and their number should be increased.

(xii) Schools should be housed in sanitary, spacious but inexpensive buildings.

(xiii) Emphasis was laid on the education of women too. Suggestions were put forth concerning special curriculum of practical utility for girls. It was clearly stated in the Resolution that too much importance should not be attached to examination in the education of girls.

(xiv) Number of women teachers and inspectors should also be increased.

(xv) The State should not completely withdraw from the sphere of secondary education.

(xvi) Further establishment of State institutions was proposed to be stopped.

(xvii) Existing institutions should continue to serve as models and proper grant-in-aid should be sanctioned to private institutions.

(xviii) An improvement in the mode of examination and curriculum was also recommended.

(xix) The Resolution provided for the expansion in university education. The existence of 5 universities and 185 colleges was considered to be insufficient in view of the vast needs and demands of the country.

(xx) The Resolution suggested that universities and high

schools should be assigned distinct spheres of activities.

(xxi) The universities should be relieved of the responsibility of granting recognition to high schools and they should be kept under Provincial Governments.

(xxii) The establishment of teaching universities was suggested by emphasising the separation of the two functions of the universities – teaching and examining.

(xxiii) Recommendations were made concerning the inclusion of subjects of industrial importance in the curriculum and provision of facilities to the students desirous of prosecuting research work.

(xxiv) The Resolution put forth certain valuable suggestions pertaining to the character formation of students and hostel life.

Evaluation of the Resolution

On account of the Outbreak of the First World War, most of the major provisions contained in the Resolution could not be carried out.

SADLER COMMISSION OR CALCUTTA UNIVERSITY COMMISSION (1917-1919)

Circumstances Leading to the Appointment of the Calcutta University Commission (1917) and Its Composition

The Resolution on Educational Policy (1913) had recommended that a university should be established for each province, the teaching activities of universities should be encouraged and that the colleges located in *mofussil* towns should be developed into teaching universities in due course. But no action could be taken by the Government primarily because of the outbreak of the Great World War. In 1917, the Government of India appointed the Calcutta University Commission which is also known as the Sadler Commission after the name of its Chairman, Dr. Michael Sadler, the Vice-

Chancellor of Leeds University. The Commission visited all university centres and after 17 months submitted its report in 13 volumes, giving a critical and comprehensive survey of educational problems. Although it deals with the Calcutta University only, the problems that it studied were more or less common to the other Indian universities. The report has greatly influenced the subsequent course of secondary and higher education in the country.

The Commission had 6 members besides the Chairman.

Terms of Reference of the Commission

To enquire into the condition and prospects of the University of Calcutta and to consider the question of a constructive policy in relation to the question it presents.

ESSENTIAL FEATURES/MAIN RECOMMENDATIONS OF THE SADLER COMMISSION

Broadly speaking, recommendations of the Commission may be studied under the following heads:

I. Recommendations Relating to Calcutta University.
II. Recommendations Relating to All Universities in India.
III. Recommendations Relating to Muslim Education.
IV. Recommendations Relating to Teacher Training.
V. Recommendations Relating to Technology.
VI. Recommendations Relating to Professional and Vocational Education.
VII. Recommendations Relating to Modern Indian Languages.
VIII. Recommendations Relating to Secondary Education

I. Recommendations Relating to Calcutta University and Its Problems

The Commission thoroughly examined the problems of the Calcutta University and reached the conclusion that the size of the University had become abnormally large and that the number of students and colleges affiliated to it had increased too much to be efficiently dealt with under a single university.

The Commission put forth three suggestions in this respect.

(i) There should be established a teaching and residential university at Dacca;

(ii) The teaching resources should be organised in Calcutta in such a way as to create a real teaching university; and

(iii) The development of *mofussil* colleges should take place in such away as to ensure the encouragement of gradual rise of university centres at a few places by concentrating all possible resources for higher education on them.

II. Recommendations Relating to All Universities

A. Important Recommendations on University Education

(i) Intermediate classes should be separated from universities and a curriculum spreading over three years should be prescribed for the degree of B.A. The stage of admission to the university was to be intermediate and not matriculation examination.

(ii) Intermediate colleges should be established for the sake of completing the first stage. These colleges should conduct teaching in arts, science, medicine, engineering, education, agriculture and commerce.

(iii) A separate High School and Intermediate Board should be formed in every province, consisting of representatives of the Government, universities, high schools and intermediate colleges, for the sake of managing secondary education. The Board should be made free from the control of the Department of Education.

(iv) The mother tongue should be used as medium of instruction in intermediate colleges.

B. Internal Administration and Organisation of Universities

The Commission expressed their general views upon the internal administration and organisation of the universities as follows:

1. The teachers of the universities should be given more powers with a view to removing unnecessary State control over them.
2. Regulations governing the working of universities should be made less rigid.
3. Provision should be made for the institution of Honours courses, as distinct from Pass course for the sake of abler students.
4. The duration of degree course should be three years after the intermediate stage.
5. For the internal administration of the university, a representative court in place of Senate and a small Executive Council in place of the syndicate should be set up.
6. A special committee should be constituted for making appointments to Professorships and Readerships. The Committee should include external experts also.
7. An Academic Council and Board of Studies be set up to settle academic questions pertaining to courses of study, examinations, degrees and research work, etc.
8. Different faculties should be created.
9. A full-time and salaried Vice-Chancellor should be appointed.
10. A Director of Physical Training should also be appointed to pay attention to the health and physical welfare of the students.

11. The Department of Education in the universities should be established and education included as a subject for the B.A. (Pass) and intermediate course.
12. It also recommended the establishment of an inter-university board for coordinating the activities of various Indian universities.

III. Recommendations Relating to Muslim Education

(i) The Muslims should be provided all educational facilities in view of their backward state in this field.

(ii) It provided for organising 'Purdah Schools' for girls upto the age of 15 or 16 years.

(iii) It empowered the Calcutta University to institute a 'Special Board of Women's Education' and set up special curriculum according to the educational needs of women.

IV. Recommendations Relating to Teacher Training

The Commission recommended that the output of trained teachers should be substantially increased.

V. Recommendations Relating to Technology

The Commission observed, "It is an important and indeed, a necessary function of the university to include applied science and technology in its courses and to recognise their systematic and practical study by degrees and diplomas".

VI. Recommendations Relating to Professional and Vocational Training

The Commission recommended that Universities must provoke provision for the efficient training in personnel needed for the industrial development of the country.

VII. Recommendations Relating to Modern Indian Languages

The Calcutta University Commission (1917) stated: "We are emphatically of opinion that there is something unsound in a system of education which leaves a young man, at the conclusion of his course, unable to speak or write his own mother tongue fluently and correctly. It is thus beyond controversy that a systematic effort must henceforth be made to promote the serious study of the vernaculars in secondary schools, intermediate colleges and in the university. The elaborate scheme recently adopted by the university for the critical, historical and comparative study of the Indian vernaculars for the M.A. examination is but the caping stone of an edifice of which the base has yet to be placed on a sound foundation, and it is only when such a structure has been completed that Bengal will have a literature worthy of the greatness and civilisation of its people."

VIII. Recommendations Relating to Secondary Education

The Commission held that reform at the stage of secondary education was essential for the improvement of university education. In this regard it made the following recommendations:

1. Separation of intermediate classes from the universities.
2. Establishment of intermediate colleges.
3. Formation of the Separate High School and Intermediate Boards.
4. Use of mother-tongue as the medium of instruction.

(These recommendations are also included under the head 'Important Recommendations on University Education' as these have a great bearing on university education also)

Implementation of the Recommendations

There were important political developments in the country in the wake of Montagu-Chelmsford Reforms (1919) under which universities were transferred to provincial government. Besides several problems arising out of the consequences of the First World War had to be given priority. Hence, the recommendations could not be put to immediate implementation. However, after the Policy Resolution of 1920, recommendations received attention. Several universities came into being.

EVALUATION OF THE SADLER REPORT : FORE-RUNNER OF THE NEW PATTERN OF EDUCATION 10+2+3.

According to A.N. Basu, "The report of the Commission contains the most comprehensive and authoritative study of the Indian education system from the secondary stage to the university. It is, therefore, quite natural that they have greatly influenced the subsequent course of secondary and higher education in the country.
('*Education in Modern India*')

In the words of Arthor Mathew, "The Report of the Calcutta University Commission has been a constant source of suggestion and information. Its significance in the History of Indian Education has been incalculable
('*The Education of India*')

When we look at the present educational scenario, we find that some of the important features find their mention in the Sadler Commission Report. The beginning of introduction of the New Pattern of Education 10+2+3 in 1975 has been hailed as a landmark in the reforms of education in India. It may be recalled that the 12 years of schooling and 3 years of degree course were recommended by the Sadler Commission (1917-1919). In this sense the Sadler Commission may be said to be the fore-runner of the present national educational structure.

Likewise the present emphasis on vocational education and technology education may be traced back to the Sadler Report.

6

Government of India Act (1935) and Wardha Scheme of Education (1937)

GOVERNMENT OF INDIA ACT (1935)

Circumstances Leading to the Act

The Congress had passed *'Purna Swaraj'* Resolution (complete Independence) and there was a growing unrest in the country. The British Government decide to impart some powers to the people of India. In this regard the Government of India Act, 1935, was an important step in the onward march of India to complete political independence. It put an end to the inherently defective diarchical system of administration, abolished the distinction between reserved and transferred departments and placed the whole field of Provincial Administration under a Ministry responsible to a legislature which had an overwhelming majority of elected members. This new system of governance, popularly known as Provincial Autonomy, came into operation in 1937 in eleven provinces of British India. With the inauguration of Provincial autonomy, earnest hopes of a great educational advance were raised. Unfortunately, these hopes did not materialise.

PROVISIONS IN THE ACT FOR EDUCATION

The Act of 1919 had made education a subject which was "partly all India, partly reserved, partly transferred with limitations, and partly transferred without limitations." The Government of India Act, 1935 improved this anomalous position considerably and divided all educational activities into two categories only—Federal (or Central) and State (or Provincial).

(a) *Federal (or Central) Subjects*

(i) The Imperial Library, Calcutta; the Indian Museum, Calcutta; the Imperial War Museum; The Victoria Memorial, Calcutta; and any similar institution controlled or financed by the Federation;

(ii) Education in the Defence Forces;

(iii) The Banaras Hindu University and the Aligarh Muslim University;

(iv) Preservation of ancient and historical monuments;

(v) Archaeology; and

(vi) Education in Centrally Administered Areas.

(b) *State (or Provincial) Subjects:* All matters regarding education of all other categories other than those included in the Federal list given above were regarded as State or Provincial subjects.

SIGNIFICANCE OF THE ACT IN THE CONTEXT OF DEVELOPMENT OF EDUCATION

The Act has a great significance from the point of view of development of education in India. Earlier there was no clear-cut area of responsibility, in the field of education. Now having a very limited area, development of education in its various dimensions and at various levels was made the responsibility of the provinces. Its positive impact was felt when under the Government of India Act (1935) responsibility was put on the provinces. In 1937, the Congress Ministries formed in nine provinces took several measures to bring about educational reforms.

The old distinction between 'reserved and transferred subjects' disappeared. The education of the Anglo-Indian and Europeans ceased to be a reserved subject.

With the beginning of Provincial Autonomy it was envisaged that there would be a rapid educational advance. Most of the difficulties which hampered the work of Indian Ministers during 1921 and 1937 disappeared.

Hopes generated through the grant of Provincial Autonomy did not materialise on account of the Second World War (1939-45). The Congress Ministries formed in 1937 lasted for less than three years. They resigned as the people of India were not taken into confidence by the British rulers while involving India in the War.

THE WARDHA SCHEME OF EDUCATION (1937)

Nomenclature of the Wardha Scheme of Education

The Wardha Scheme of Education derives its name from the education conference of National Workers held at Wardha under the presidentship of Mahatma Gandhi. The scheme is also known as Nai Talim/Basic Education/Buniyadi Talim (Shiksha)/Basic Shiksha.

The scheme is the outcome of the philosophy of Gandhiji. It was given a definite shape by the Committee under the chairmanship of Dr. Zakir Hussain who later on became the President of India.

ORIGIN OF THE SCHEME

Gandhiji found the main defects of the system of education as, "I am fully convinced that the present system of education is not only wasteful but positively harmful. They pick up evil habits. English has created a permanent bar between the highly educated few and the uneducated many." He further said, "Let us now cry a halt and concentrate on educating the child properly through manual work not as a side activity but as a prime means of intellectual activity."

The scheme was the outcome of the sound thinking of Gandhiji. Perhaps Gandhiji is the only freedom fighter in the world who initiated and strengthened several constructive programmes for the economic, educational and social development of the people. He considered education as an effective instrument of national reconstruction.

Gandhiji emphasised the self-sufficiency aspect of education along with other aspects. In fact he wanted India to be self-sufficient in every walk of national life.

In July 1937, Gandhiji wrote in the *Harijan*, "By education, I mean an all-round drawing out of the best in child and man — body, mind and spirit ... Literacy itself is no education, I would, therefore, begin the child's education by teaching it a useful handicraft and enabling it to produce from the moment it begins its training. Thus every school can be made self-supporting, the condition being that the State takes over the manufacture of these schools."

Conference of National Workers

The same year, in October, a Conference of National Workers was called at Wardha under the presidentship of Mahatma Gandhi and, after considering his ideas, passed the following resolutions.

1. That in the opinion of this Conference, free and compulsory education be provided for seven years on a nation-wide scale;
2. That the medium of instruction be the mother tongue;
3. That the Conference endorses the proposal, made by Mahatma Gandhi, that the process of education throughout this period should centre round some productive form of manual work, and that all other

abilities to be developed or training to be given should, as far as possible, be integrally related to the central handicraft chosen with due regard to the environment of the child;

4. That the Conference expects that the system of education will be gradually able to cover the remuneration of the teachers.

Appointment of a Committee

This Conference appointed a committee of distinguished educationists under the chairmanship of Dr. Zakir Hussain to prepare a detailed syllabus. Among others who served on the Committee, Prof. K.G. Saiyidain's name is prominent. The report of the Committee published in March 1938, has come to be known as the Wardha Scheme of Education. It was approved by Mahatma Gandhi and was placed before the Indian National Congress at its Haripura Session held in March 1938. The Congress accepted the scheme.

WARDHA SCHEME OF EDUCATION AT A GLANCE

The fundamental features of the scheme which was evolved in due course are as follows:

1. A school of say 5½ hours could roughly be divided on the following basis:

Physical activities ...	20 minutes
Mother Tongue ...	20 minutes
Social Studies & General Science ...	60 minutes
Art ...	40 minutes
Arithmetic ...	20 minutes
Craft work including study of correlated subjects ...	2½ hours
Thus the craft work will have 2½ hours instead of ...	3 hrs & 20 min.

2. Free and compulsory education to be given for 8 years

(from 6 to 14 years) in two stages, instead of 7 to 14. The junior stage covering five years and the senior 3 years.

3. The medium of instruction is to be the mother tongue.
4. Education is to centre round some form of productive work. The social and physical environment to be used for correlation in addition to craft.
5. The self-supporting aspect is not to be over-emphasised. The sale-proceeds of the finished goods should be able to help the school to cover some part of its expenditure.
6. External examinations are to be abolished. The day-to-day work of the students is to be the determining factor.
7. Text books to be avoided as far as possible.
8. Cleanliness and health, citizenship, play and recreation are to be given sufficient importance.

EVALUATION OF THE WARDHA SCHEME OF EDUCATION

Merits of Wardha Scheme

I. *Craft Work in Schools*: Modern educational thought is practically unanimous in commending the idea of educating children through some suitable form of productive work. This method is considered to be the most effective approach to the problem of providing an integral all-sided education. It is useful on account of the following:

(1) Psychologically, it is desirable, because it relieves the child from the tyranny of a purely academic and theoretical instruction against which its active nature is always making a healthy protest. It balances the intellectual and practical elements of experience, and may be made an instrument of educating the body and the mind in coordination.

(2) Socially considered, the introduction of such practical productive work in education, to be participated in by all the children of the nation, will tend to break down

the existing barriers of prejudice between manual and intellectual workers, harmful alike for both. It will also cultivate in the only possible way a true sense of the dignity of labour and of human solidarity – an ethical and moral gain of incalculable significance.

(3) Economically considered, carried out intelligently and efficiently, the scheme will increase the productive capacity of our workers and will also enable them to utilise their leisure advantageously.

(4) From the strictly educational point of view greater concreteness and reality can be given to the knowledge acquired by children by making some significant craft the basis of education. Knowledge will thus become related to life, and its various aspects will be correlated with one another.

II. *Activity Curriculum*: In order to work out an effective and natural coordination of the various subjects and to make the syllabus a means of adjusting the child intelligently and actively to his environment, the Wardha Scheme laid stress on three centres, intrinsically inter-connected, as the foci for the curriculum, i.e., the Physical Environment, the Social Environment, and Craft Work, which is their natural meeting point since it utilises the resources of the former for the purpose of the latter.

The Wardha Scheme of Education attempted to draft an 'activity curriculum', which implies that our schools must be places of work, experimentation and discovery, not of passive absorption of information imparted at second hand. It stressed this principle by advocating that all teaching should be carried on through concrete life situations relating to craft or to social and physical environment, so that whatever a child learns becomes assimilated into his growing activity.

III. *Learning by Doing*: Learning by doing sums up the educational methods of basic education. It is absolutely wrong to think that true education is acquired from books alone. There are other methods and sources which are more helpful in acquiring true knowledge. 'Chalk' and 'Talk' lessons are also not very useful. All educationists have condemned bookish knowledge. Gandhiji believed that school must be a 'doing thing'. In basic system of education children acquire the knowledge of the formal school subjects as a bye-product of purposeful activities.

IV. *Social Activities and Community Life*: The corner-stone of Basic education lies in the activities and the community life of the school. Apart from craft, productive activities and occupations find an important place in the curriculum of a basic school. Living together and doing together is the soul of any progressive system of education and Basic system fully incorporates this in its curriculum and methods of teaching.

V. *Self-Sufficiency*: Gandhiji felt that the educational system as introduced by the foreigners in India was expensive and it was very difficult for a poor country like India to spread education if it followed that system. So Gandhiji went a step further and declared that the New Education must not only be work-centred but must also be self-supporting.

"... You have to start with the conviction that looking to the need of the villages of India our rural education ought to be made self-supporting if it is to be compulsory. This education ought to be for the a kind of insurance against unemployment.

Not only from economic point of view, this education must be self-sufficient, but also from social and moral points of view. This means that at the end of the period of basic education the individual should become self-reliant and self-supporting."

VI. *Modification of the Views of Mahatma Gandhi on Self-Sufficiency*: Dr. Zakir Hussain Committee pointed out the danger of overdoing of craft work and warned that oral work, drawing and expression work should not be lost sight of. The educative aspect is more important than the economic aspect. It thus shifted the emphasis from complete support to partial self-support. It was felt that with the earnings through sale of craft products, uniform for the students or mid-day meal or purchase of some necessary equipment may be made.

Free and Compulsory Education: Seven year's free and compulsory education is one of the fundamentals of this scheme and this cardinal principle has been emphasised due to two reasons:

1. India is a democratic country and success of democracy depends upon the enlightened citizens. Our great leaders like Gokhale worked for the introduction of compulsory education for a long time. In is historic speech, Gokhale said that if elementary education was to spread in India, it must be made compulsory and if it was to be compulsory it must be free.
2. Gandhiji's dream of a classless society, free of exploitation – economic and social – can be realised only if everyone is educated.

VII. *Mother Tongue as Medium of Instruction*: It is now universally recognised that the young child can learn with great facility if the medium of instruction is its mother tongue. Gandhiji asserted that no education is possible through foreign medium and all elementary education must be imparted through the medium of the mother tongue.

VIII. *Education Through Correlation*: Correlation is one of the important features and crux of Basic education. In this scheme of education, Gandhiji wished to give knowledge as a compact whole. The modern educationists also advocate this. The Basic education is therefore, an effort to correlate the life of the child with his immediate, physical and social environment. It is an effort to make knowledge easier and at the same time more meaningful.

IX. *Integrated Knowledge*: Basic education treats knowledge as an integrated whole. Curriculum is built round three integrally related centres: (i) Physical environment, (ii) Social environment, and (iii) Craft work.

X. *Relationship with Life*: A Basic School must become an active environment where teaching is not cut off from the life of the miniature community of the school and the community itself. Education is to be directed to the needs of life. It is not to pursue an idea which has no relation with or is totally isolated from the real situations of life.

XI. *Training in Citizenship*: Basic education aims at developing ideas of mutual understanding and habits of cooperative and mutually helpful living among the students through its various practical and constructive programmes. The new education aims at giving the citizens of the future a keen sense of personal warmth, dignity and efficiency. It is likely to strengthen in them the desire for self-improvement and social service in a cooperative community.

XII. *Greater Freedom for the Teacher and the Taught*: In Basic education discipline does not mean order and external restraint but an intelligent use of freedom. The teacher gets many opportunities to make experiments, think for himself and put his ideas and plans into practice.

XIII. *Basic Education is Not a Class Education*: The ultimate objective of Basic education is to create a social order in which there is no unnatural division between 'haves' and 'have-nots' and every one is assured of a living wage and the right to freedom.

XIV. *Basic Education in the Rural as well as Urban Areas*: It is wrong to assume that Basic education is intended to be imparted in the rural area only. "In fact, in one sense there is a greater need for Basic education in urban areas than in rural areas. In rural areas the children who participate in the life of the farm or allied occupation of their families have certain types of further education. In performing their jobs the children come into direct contact with actual life and the experience they get forms the basis of further education. On the other hand, in large towns and big industrial cities the children miss the opportunities for rich experiences and direct contact with life", observed Dr. K.L. Shrimali.

Significance of the Word 'Basic'

One. The word 'Basic' is derived from the word 'Base' which means the bottom or the foundation of a thing upon which the whole thing rests or is made.

Two. It is basic because it is based on ancient Indian culture.

Three. It is basic because it lays down the minimum educational standards which every Indian child is entitled to receive without any distinction of caste or creed.

Four. It is basic because it is closely related to the basic needs and interests of the child.

Five. It is basic because it makes use of the native potentialities of the child.

Six. It is basic because it is intimately related to the basic occupations of the community.

Seven. It is basic because it is for the common man of the country, who is the foundation and the backbone of our national life.

Eight. It is basic because it comes first in time, i.e., it is the primary period of one's education.

Criticism of Basic Education

1. *Unsound Psychological Foundations of Wardha Scheme of Education*: "The delicate but inexorable laws governing the development of the tender mind of the child have been completely ignored. The child is treated just as a policeman or a soldier, merely as a unit in a homogeneous mass. His individuality is ignored. He is viewed merely as a means to an

end – the end being earning capacity and citizenship of sorts." *P.S. Naidu*

"Play is the only means by which creative energy can be released. Enlightened and informed educational opinion all over the civilised world is decidedly against forcing the child to learn a craft before he is twelve plus. It is nothing short of cruelty to make the child earn an anna or half an anna per hour during the stage when he ought to be playing and enjoying himself." *P.S. Naidu*

"There are three aspects of human nature – cognitive, affective and conative. The Wardha Scheme emphasises the last aspect piously hoping that the student will willy-nilly get trained in the first through his training in the last. The middle aspect is completely ignored." *P.S. Naidu*

2. *Undue Emphasis on Craft as the Only Basis of Correlation*: "It is impossible to establish any natural association between craft and all the subjects of cultural value which any sane system of education should cover through its curriculum. Teaching should be concrete and should be based on the child's active experience in his environment. But it is absurd to hang all knowledge from the peg of a single craft." *P.S. Naidu*

3. *No Place for Religious Education*: "Education suited to our national genius should have definite religious bias, with contempt of worldly pursuits in its core. Craft-centred education is decidedly alien to our ancient ideals." *P.S. Naidu*

4. *Basic Education Not Suited in an Age of Industrialisation*: As ours is a system of education which claims to produce an integrated individual, the emphasis on craft is out of place in a community which has its face turned towards developing its economy to the full. So far Basic education failed to relate to the economic policy of the State. But if this point is ignored, we shall find ourselves burdened with an educational system which turns out misfits even more rapidly than the one with which we are so dissatisfied." *S. Natarajan*

"With rapid industrialisation of India, knowledge of science and mathematics may become more desirable than skill in handicrafts." Editorial, *Educational Review*

5. *Ruinous Competition*: "This scheme will hit the professional artisans hard by creating ruinous competitions." *P.S. Naidu*

6. *Deficient Working of Basic Schools*: There is some loss in mechanical arithmetic and spelling; lack of sufficient intensive and repetitive drill." *J. Lahri*

"Two types of basic education have ultimately crystallised: the Orthodox Wardha type of eight years craft-centred basic schools and the more liberal craft-based but activity type of basic schools in two stages, viz., Junior Basic stage 6 to 11 plus and Senior Basic stage upto 14 plus with the result that at the moment we find two types sponsored by the different stages." *J. Lahri*

7. *Neglect of the Child*: "In a hurry to pay more attention to craft, it has neglected the child." *Anath Nath Basu*

"Basic education is looked upon more as a social and economic duty than as a joyful adventure." *Anath Nath Basu*

"Craft is only a slogan, a fiction, which is practised on ceremonial occasions for the benefit of visitors." *R.K. Singh*

8. *Faulty Time-table*: "In a basic school only two-thirds or half the normal time is given to academic education, the rest being taken up by crafts. And further, since on the time-table academic subjects generally come after the craft work, mostly agriculture, students are sometimes too tired to take to academic work kindly." *R.K. Singh*

9. *No Dexterity in Any Craft*: "Students spend one-third or half the time for craft work without acquiring any dexterity worth speaking of in any craft." *R.K. Singh*

Some Epithets Attached with Basic System of Education

1. Basic Education is a *Fad*: It has no sound psychological

and pedagogical basis.

2. Basic Education is a *Fallacy*: The very fundaments are wrong and not properly conceived.
3. Basic Education is a *Farce*: The scheme is impracticable. Traditional methods are still followed. The craft materials are just stored and a show is put up, whenever there are visitors.
4. Basic Education is a *Fraud*: Is being committed on the nation by those who are in power. It is a sort of political stunt to play with the sentiments of the people.

Promotion of Basic Education: Such type of criticism became the order of the day even during the life time of Gandhiji. Several attempts were made to remove misgivings about basic education after Independence when it was accepted as the national system of education at the primary stage. Overnight all primary schools were declared as basic schools irrespective of the equipment and the necessary facilities for craft work.

During the First Three Five Year Plan, serious efforts were made by the Government for the promotion of basic education. Still it could not become popular.

Death Knel of Basic Education: Its Relevance Today

The Education Commission 1964-66, popularly known as the Kothari Commission went into all aspects of education at all levels. Although it considered the 'movement of basic education as a landmark in the history of education in India', it gave a call for the 'reorientation of basic education programme in view of the changed character and need of the society'. It popularised the concept of 'work experience'.

After the publication of the report of the Commission, the term basic education was almost 'banished'.

The National Institute of Basic Education set up by the Government of India, which functioned as an important department of the NCERT for the purpose of research, extension and training was rounded up.

The Government of India's Resolution on National Policy on Education (1968) did not mention the term 'basic education'. It declared 'work experience' as an integral part of education.

The Ishwar Bhai Patel Committee (1977), and the Adiseshiah Committee (1978) used the term 'Socially Useful Productive Work (SUPW)'.

Again in the National Policy of Education (1986 and as modified in 1992), there is no mention of Basic System of Education.

It must, however, be admitted that the emphasis on Basic Education led to the popularisation of 'Vocationalisation of Education'. It appears the Basic System of Education or the Wardha Scheme of Education is confined to the pages of history.

7

Sargent Report (1944)

NOMENCLATURE OF THE SARGENT REPORT

It was the first comprehensive educational plan formulated by the Central Advisory Board of Education. It is popularly known as the Sargent Report, after the name of John Sargent, Educational Adviser to the government of India. Sir Jogendra Singh was the Chairman of the Committee which had 22 other members. The report is also known as the Post War Education Development Plan or the Report of the CABE. The plan aimed at tackling the problems of education as a whole. In fact the work on educational planning in India had already started in 1938 when a National Planning Committee had been set up to take up educational restructuring at the national level. However, the Second World War interrupted the work. The Central Advisory Board of Education (CABE) had also taken up the work in 1938 but the finalisation of the reports of various Committees could be done only in 1943-44. The Report envisaged that India would reach the educational standard of the England of 1939 in a period of not less than 40 years.

The Report significantly quoted the White Paper on Education of England: "Upon the education of the people of this country the fate of this country depends." It revealed that whereas the pre-war Britain was spending Rs.33.20 per head on education, India's comparable expenditure was only Rs.0.89 per head. It championed basic education for children from 6 to 14 and pleaded for effective teaching at the primary level. It found that a national system of education would take 30 to 40 years to be evolved.

ACCEPTANCE OF THE BASIC SYSTEM OF EDUCATION

The Report observed: "Basic (primary and middle) education as envisaged by the Central Advisory Board, embodies many of the educational ideas contained in the original Wardha Scheme, though it differs from it in certain important particulars. The main principle of learning through activity has been endorsed by educationists all over the world. At the lower stages the activity will take many forms, leading gradually upto a basic craft or crafts suited to local conditions. So far as possible the whole of the curriculum will be harmonised with this general conception. The three R's by themselves can no longer be regarded as an adequate equipment for efficient citizenship. The Board, however, is unable to endorse the view that education at any stage and particularly in the lowest stages can or should be expected to pay for itself through the sale of articles produced by the pupils. The most which can be expected in this respect is that sales should cover the cost of the additional materials and equipment required for practical work.

'Basic' education, while preserving its essential unity, will consist of two stages – the junior (or primary) stage, covering a period of five years and the senior (or middle) stage, covering three years. Those who find the term 'basic' unattractive and prefer the existing nomenclature of 'primary' and 'middle' for these two stages are of course at liberty to retain these, provided they accept the essential unity of the two stages and the necessity of so planning the primary course that it leads up naturally to the middle."

CHIEF FEATURES AND MAJOR RECOMMENDATIONS OF THE SARGENT REPORT

1. Nursery Education/Pre-Primary Basic Education

(a) An adequate provision of pre-primary instruction in the form of Nursery Schools or classes is an essential adjunct to any national system of education.

(b) In urban areas, where sufficient children are available within a reasonable radius, separate Nursery Schools or departments may be provided; elsewhere Nursery classes should be attached to Junior Basic (Primary) Schools.

(c) Nursery Schools and classes should, invariably be staffed with women teachers who have received special training for this work.

(d) Pre-primary education should in all cases be free.

(e) The main object of education at this stage is to give young children social experience rather than formal instruction.

2. Basic Education

(a) A system of universal, compulsory and free education for all boys an girls between the ages of six and fourteen should be introduced as speedily as possible though in view of the practical difficulty of recruiting the requisite supply of trained teachers it may not be possible to complete it in less than forty years.

(b) The Senior Basic (Middle) School, being the finishing school for the great majority of future citizens, is of fundamental importance and should be generously staffed and equipped.

3. High School Education

(a) For bright children high schools should provide a course covering six years and the normal age of admission should be about eleven.

(b) Entry to High Schools should be on a selective basis; only those pupils should be admitted who show promise of taking full advantage of the education provided.

(c) High Schools should be of two types – (i) Academic, and (ii) Technical. The objective of both should be to provide a good all-round education combined with some preparation in the later stages for the careers which pupils will enter on leaving school.

4. University Education

(a) In order to raise standards all round, the conditions for admission must be revised with the object of ensuring that all students are capable of taking full advantage of a University Course. Adequate financial assistance must be provided for poor students.

(b) The present intermediate course should be abolished. Ultimately the whole of this course should be covered in the High School but as an immediate step the first year of the course should be transferred to High School and the second to Universities.

(c) The minimum length of a University degree course should be three yeas.

5. Technical, Commercial and Art Education

In view of the prospective needs of post-war industry and commerce for skilled technicians, and in order to cater for the aptitudes of those who will derive greater benefit from a practical course, the establishment of an efficient system of technical education at all stages, is a matter of great urgency.

6. Adult Education

(a) To secure an early and effective solution of India's educational problems, the provision of facilities for adult education on the widest scale and the introduction of a free and compulsory system of primary education are of equal urgency and must be treated as complementary to one another.

(b) Literacy is a means to further education and must not be regarded as an end in itself.

(c) Efforts should be directed in the beginning to persuade illiterates voluntarily to undergo instruction.

(d) In a movement of this character the utmost freedom must be allowed to experiment and regard must be had at all times to local conditions.

(e) The form in which instruction is given must be intelligible and interesting to the student and the instruction itself should be closely related to his occupation, his personal interests and the social and economic conditions under which he lives.

7. Training of Teachers

(a) New Training Colleges (including University Education Departments) must be provided to supply the additional teachers whom a national system will require.

(b) Arrangements should be made to pick out suitable boys and girls towards the end of the high school course. This is particularly important in girls' high schools in view of the vast increase in the number of women teachers required.

(c) The courses provided should be essentially practical and should be specially related to the needs of the schools in which the trainees will subsequently serve.

(d) No fees should be charged in training college; liberal assistance should be available for the maintenance of poor students.

(e) Refresher courses are of the utmost important and should be provided for all types of teachers but particularly for those in remote rural areas. Facilities should be provided for research and selected teachers should be encouraged to study educational methods in foreign country.

(f) No teacher should receive less than Rs.20 per mensem.

8. Aims and Objects of a School Medical Service

It is absolutely essential that steps be taken to ensure that children attending school are healthy and kept healthy. This is necessary not only from the medical but also from the educational point of view.

Probably fifty percent of the children attending school would be found to require medical attention or medical observation.

9. Education of the Handicapped

Provision for the mentally or physically handicapped should form an essential part of a national system of education and should be administered by the Education Department.

10. Female Education

Suitable courses should be framed for girls attending senior level schools which should include such subjects as cookery, laundry work, needle work, home crafts, the care of children and first aid, the remainder of the instruction to be correlated with this course of domestic science in accordance with the general principles of the 'basic education' scheme.

Special stress should be laid on the training of women teachers.

11. Medium of Instruction

The medium of instruction should be the mother tongue of the pupils.

12. Common Language

A common language for India is desirable. This should be Hindustani with both the Urdu and Hindi scripts. Option should be given to children to choose the script, and provision should be made for teaching them in that script. Every teacher should know both scripts, viz., Urdu and Hindi.

13. Recreation and Social Activities

(a) The provision of recreation and social activities on an adequate scale is an essential feature of any modern educational system.

(b) A youth movement should aim at co-ordinating and supplementing rather than superseding the work of organisations already dealing with aspects of this problem.

14. Employment Bureau

Employment Bureau should form an essential part of educational administration. They are especially necessary in India in view of the restricted openings at the moment for providing employment.

15. Administration

The provinces should remain the main units for educational administration except in regard to University and higher technical education the activities of which should be coordinated on an All-India basis.

TARGETS

1. It was spread over a period of 40 years (1945-84).
2. An annual expenditure of Rs.3,126 million to be incurred on the then estimated population of 290 million; i.e., Rs.11/- per head of population at the 1939 prices.
3. Provision of facilities for one child in every 21 at the pre-primary stage.
4. Free and compulsory education on basic lines for all children in the age-group 6-11.
5. Compulsory senior basic education for three years for four-fifths of children in the age group 11-14.
6. Secondary education for selected and gifted children (for one child out of every five who completed the primary course).

7. University education for one out of every fifteen students who completed the secondary school.
8. A fair sized programme of technical education and the provision of other ancillary services.
9. Liquidation of adult illiteracy.

Financial Details

The Report thus estimated that the total annual expenditure on the educational system proposed by it would come to Rs. 3126 million out of which a sum of about Rs. 356 million (or about 11%) would come from fees and other sources and the balance of Rs. 2770 million (or about 89%) would have to be provided from public taxation. The details of these estimates can be seen at a glance in the following table.

(*Rs. in millions*)

		Estimated gross annual expenditure	*Estimated income from sources other than public funds*	*Estimated net expenditure to be met from public funds*
1.	Basic (Primary and Middle) Education	2,000	—	2,000
2.	Pre-Primary Education	32	—	32
3.	High School Education	790	290	500
4.	University Education	96	29	67
5.	Technical, Commercial and Art Education	100	20	80
6.	Adult Education	30	—	30
7.	Training of Teachers	62	17	45
8.	School Medical Service	—	—	—
9.	Education of the Handicapped	—	—	—
10.	Recreative and Social Activities	10	—	10
11.	Employment Bureau	6	—	6
12.	Administration	—	—	—
	Total	3,126	356	2,770

Valuable Report: K.G. Saiyidain, an eminent educationist

considered the report very valuable on account of the following:

First, it was the first comprehensive scheme of national education.

Second, it emphasised equality of opportunity.

Third, it appreciated the importance of the teaching profession and advocated better salary and status for teachers.

Saiyidain explained the merits of the Sargent Scheme in these words.

"What is the wider significance of this scheme? It is the first comprehensive scheme of national education; it does not start with the assumption, implicit in all previous Government schemes, that India was destined to occupy a position of educational inferiority in comparison of other nations; it is based on the conviction that what other countries have achieved in the field of education is well within the competence of this country. The mere formulation of such a scheme ensures that no other scheme which proposes any half-hearted, piecemeal changes or merely tinkers with the idea of expansion can even be seriously entertained.

"Secondly, it is inspired by the desire to provide equality of opportunity at different stages of education. At the primary stage it envisages not merely the provision of free schooling but also of other facilities without which the poorer children cannot fully avail themselves of the educational opportunities—mid-day meal, books, scholarships, medical inspection and treatment. At higher stages, free places and scholarships are proposed for all bright and deserving students. This is by no means the full measure of education equality which an enlightened sense of social justice demands, but it is certainly a welcome step forward towards that goal and would be a great improvement on the existing situation.

"Thirdly, it stresses in clear terms the importance of the

teaching profession and makes proposals for increasing its miserable standard of salaries and poor conditions of service. It lays down a minimum national scale of salaries, and provides for its adjustment in accordance with the rise in the cost of living. The national scale has already been accepted and given effect to in many Provinces (with certain modifications, not always favourable to teachers, but it has not had as bracing and stimulating an effect on the profession as was expected, because the rise in prices has been quicker and steeper than the rise in salaries."

Criticism of the Report

Syed Nurullah and J.P. Naik have pointed out the following points of criticism of the Sargent Report:

1. It placed a very tame objective before the nation.
2. Its financial applications had not been worked out carefully.
3. It was based on the British ideals and pattern.

They explained their criticism as, "It placed a very tame idea before the country. As the report itself admitted, India would reach the educational standard of the England of 1939 in a period of not less than 40 years. In other words, even assuming that the plan was fully implemented, the India of 1984 would still be nearly 50 years behind England. This idea did not naturally satisfy any ardent educationist."

"The financial implications of the Report also came in for a good deal of comment. The cost of working out the scheme would come to about Rs. 313 crores, on the basis of the population of India as it was in 1940. If allowances were made for the growth of population during the time that would be required to implement this scheme, and for the rise in the standard of life and cost of living the total cost of the scheme would be in the order of Rs. 1,000/- crores per annum. Even assuming that large-scale developments in industry and agriculture would be introduced and that the standard of income of the people would rise, it appeared doubtful if India could afford this huge expenditure. It was, therefore, opined that, on financial grounds, the scheme is too Utopian to be practicable."

"It has been pointed out that the only ideal held up by the Report is that of the educational system of England. While as a matter of fact, England is the one country which could not very well serve as a model to India, because the social, political and economic conditions in the two countries are so vastly different – If India had to have a model, she could look for it elsewhere in eastern countries like China or Egypt or Turkey or in Western agricultural countries like Denmark or Soviet Russia, all of which had many problems similar to those of India, and which have been able to achieve splendid results in a very short time."

Concluding Observations

Educational planning in independent India started in 1951 with the setting of the Planning Commission. At present we are on the threshold of the Tenth Five Year Plan. Results of the planning during all these years reveal that Sargent Plan was not unrealistic from financial and other points of view. A good deal of criticism of the plan was based on theoretical considerations and distrust of the foreign rulers. Our own achievements in the field of universalisation have not been encouraging. We have failed to fulfil our obligations to the Article 45 of the Constitution. We are far behind the targets.

According to the Article 45 of the Constitution, India was expected to realise the objective of free and compulsory education for all children until they complete the age of fourteen years within a period of fifteen years from the commencement of the Constitution. In other words, the target year was 1960. Target date has been revised from time to time;

first to 1970 then to 1976 and later to 1990. The National Policy on Education (NPE) fixed the date as 1995. The '*Sarva Shiksha Abhiyan*' launched in 2001-2002, fixed the year 2010 as the target date. Keeping in view these facts, it is observed that the Sargent Report was not unrealistic and did not place the tame objective before the nation.

8

Overview of the System of Education During the British Rule

INTRODUCTION

No National System of Education

At the very outset, it must be pointed out that the system of education in India was developed primarily and predominantly in the light of the economic, political, religious and social developments taking place in England. As observed by Dr. Aparna Basu in '*Essays in the History of Indian Education*' (1982), "The East India's primary education aim was to turn out clerks who could be employed cheaply; the (English) Free Traders hoped that English educated Indians would develop a taste for the products of Lancashire. For the missionaries, the new education was the first step towards the conversion of Indians to Christianity. To the (English) Liberals, what was important was the civilising and human influence; aim of education was to form "a class of persons, Indians in blood and colour but English' in tastes, in opinions, in morals and intellect", "a class which would serve as interpreters between the government and the millions whom it governed."

The British rulers began to take a keen interest in education since 1813. Earlier, the missionaries and the officials of the East India Company in their personal capacity promoted education.

In 1781, the Calcutta '*Madrasah*' was formed by Warren

Hastings 'to qualify the sons of Mohammadan gentlemen for responsible and lucrative offices in the State, and to produce competent officers for Courts of Justice."

In 1791, the Banaras Sanskrit College was established by Jonathan Duncan, the Resident at Banaras to conciliate the Hindu population of the newly acquired territories of the Company. Incidentally this was in accordance with the political consideration of the policy of 'Divide and Rule' of the British.

The British System of Education did not develop a national system of education which is a means to an end and can only be organised as a corollary to the role which a nation is expected to play. According to Nurullah and Naik, "The imperialistic nature of the British power prevented it from visualising a self-respecting and independent India. The missionaries looked upon her as a recruiting ground for Christianity; the company generally regarded her as a field for commerce and profits; the Despatch of 1854 referred to her as the producer of raw materials or the buyer of the finished products of British industries; Curzon considered her as an eternal field for the civilising influence of the British administration; and until the end of the Second World War, all declarations of official policy were characterised by the same blind refusal to visualise India as a sovereign, independent nation with her own unique and valuable contribution to make the universal culture. There is obviously no room for a national system of education within the four corners of such an imperialist political philosophy."

PHASES OF DEVELOPMENT OF EDUCATION IN INDIA DURING THE BRITISH RULE (1800-1947): POLICY DOCUMENTS AND COMMITTEES AND COMMISSIONS

The period was marked by policy decisions. Several Committees and Commissions on education were also appointed to make recommendations on the improvement of Education in India.

Following were the phases of the development of education in India during the British rule.

First Phase – Beginning of State Policy (1813): The Charter Act of 1813, for the first time the East India Company made an annual provision for a sum of not less than one lakh of rupees for the promotion of learning. It was admitted by the British Parliament for the first time that 'education in India had a claim on public revenues'.

Second Phase – Oriental-Occidental Controversy (1823-1835): The parties to the controversies were the' Orientalists' or 'Classicists' and 'Occidentalists' or 'Anglicists'. The former were in favour of educating the upper classes of the Indian people through the medium of their classical languages and the latter through the medium of English.

Third Phase – Macaulay's Minute: The famous minute of Lord Macaulay, the first Law Member of the Governor-General's Executive Council, submitted in 1835, opened a new chapter in the educational history of India. (*For details see chapter 1*)

Fourth Phase – Bentinck's Proclamation: This was Resolution (order) dated March 7, 1835 of Lord William Bentinck consequent to the acceptance of Macaulay's Minute.

This was the first declaration of the British Government in the field of education in India. It eventually determined the aim, content and the medium of instruction in India. Promotion of western sciences and art was acknowledged as the avowed object.

Schools teaching European literature and science became popular because of the great interest shown in English education by some of the educated Indians and more particularly by leaders like Raja Rammohan Roy and others.

Fifth Phase – Auckland's Minute (1839): In this minute Lord Auckland, the Governor-General, after studying the causes of the dispute between the 'Orientalists' and the 'Occidentalists' tried to satisfy both the parties and outlined the future policy of the Government: (i) Existing Oriental colleges may continue and receive the same grant as they were receiving previous to Bentinck's Minute; (ii) Existing Oriental colleges may start English classes if they so desired; (iii) One-fourth of the students of these colleges may receive scholarships; (iv) Books of instruction in Oriental languages may be published out of funds sanctioned for Oriental education.

Sixth Phase – Wood's Despatch (1854): The despatch was issued in 1854 by Sir Charles Wood (afterwards Lord Halifax), the President of the Board of Control in India, in which he declared 'the education that we desire to see extended in India is that which has for its object the diffusion of the improved arts, sciences, philosophy and literature of Europe, in short of European knowledge'. (*For details see chapter 3*)

Seventh Phase – Indian Education Commission (1882) *or the Hunter Commission*: The Commission was appointed in 1882 by Lord Ripon under the Chairmanship of William Hunter to enquire particularly into the manner in which effect had been given to the principles of the Despatch of 1854 and to suggest measures for carrying out the policy as laid down therein.

The Commission failed to see the financial implications of its recommendations. However, the historical value of this document is incalculable. It is also known as Hunter Commission.

During the period 1882-1902, there was a considerable expansion in the field of secondary education.

Eighth Phase – Lord Curzon's Period and the University Commission of 1902: The Commission was appointed by Lord Curzon in 1992 'to inquire into the conditions and prospects of the universities established in India, to consider and report upon any proposals which have been or may be made for improving their constitution and working; and to recommend to the Governor-General-in-Council such measures as may tend to elevate standard of universities teaching, and to promote the advancement of learning'.

Resolution of the Government on Education (1904): The educational policy was declared in the form of a government resolution on 11th March 1904 by Lord Curzon.

Ninth Phase – Gokhale's Resolution in the Imperial Legislative Council on Primary Education (1911): The Bill was introduced in the Imperial Legislative Council on 16th March, 1911 by Gopal Krishna Gokhale, a member of the Council, 'to provide for the gradual introduction of the principle of compulsion into the elementary education of the country'. On March 17, 1912 the Bill was rejected by 38 votes to 13.

Tenth Phase – Resolution of the Government of India on Education (1913): The Resolution advocated three cardinal principles of educational policy – (1) Instead of increasing the number of existing institutions their standard should be raised; (2) The curricula of primary and secondary schools should be made more practical and useful; (3) Facilities of higher studies and research should be provided in India so that Indian students may not have to go abroad.

Eleventh Phase – Calcutta University Commission (1917-1919): The Commission was appointed by the Government of India in 1917 under the Chairmanship of Dr. Michael Sadler, the Vice-Chancellor of the University of Leeds, 'to enquire into the conditions and prospects of the University of Calcutta and to consider the question of a constructive policy in relation to the question it represents'.

The Report of the Commission became a constant source of suggestion and information. It greatly influenced the subsequent course of secondary and higher education in the country.

Twelfth Phase – National Movement in Education (1905-1921): The movement demanded national education which became more pressing with the growth of the national movement during the early part of the 20th century.

Thirteenth Phase – Education under Diarchy (1921-1937): Education was treated as a transferred subject under a diarchical system of government in the provinces of India, introduced in 1921 as a result of the Government of India Act, 1919 passed by the British Parliament. Subjects of administration were divided into two categories, i.e., Reserved and Transferred Subjects. The reserved subjects were put under the Governor and his executive council and the transferred subjects under the ministers who were responsible to the Provincial Legislature. Education was made transferred subject and the development of education was the responsibility of the Minister for Education. Finance was a reserved subject with the result that the Education Minister had to face many difficulties. Moreover, the Education Minister had no control over the I.C.S. officers whose services were controlled by the Secretary of the State for India.

Fourteenth Phase – Hartog Committee (1928): The Committee was appointed by the Simon Commission in 1928 under the Chairmanship of Sir Philip Hartog to review the position of education in India. It regretted the slow progress of literacy and a high percentage of failure at the Matriculation Examination which dominated the secondary education. It recommended that there should be more diversified curricula in the schools.

Fifteenth Phase – Education under Provincial Autonomy and Congress Ministries (1937-39): The Government of India Act 1935, divided all educational activities into two categories Federal: (or Central) and State (or Provincial).

The Congress Ministries formed in 1937 undertook several steps for the promotion of Basic System of Education propounded by Gandhiji.

Sixteenth Phase (1939-1947): With the resignation of Congress Ministries in 1939 on the eve of the First World War, the new system of education received a set back.

The British rulers made two attempts after 1935 to introduce changes in the system of education. However on account of War, the reports and plans remained on paper. Since these are of some interest, they are given here in the summary form.

1. *Abbot Wood Report* (1937): The Report was submitted in 1937 by the two expert Advisers – A. Abbot, Ex-Chief Inspector of Technical Schools, Board of Education, England and S.H. Wood, Director of Intelligence, Board of Education, England – invited by the Government of India in 1936 on the recommendation of the Central Advisory Board of Education to advise 'whether any vocational or practical training should be imparted in primary, secondary and higher secondary schools, and if so, what should be its nature and extent'. The report consisted of two parts: (i) Report on Vocational Education written by Mr. A. Abbot, and (ii) Report on General Education written by Mr. S.H. Wood. The report stressed that vocational education was as important as general education. "Neither of them can claim to be more useful and necessary. If general education brings about the development of the non-material culture of a country, vocational education does the same thing for material culture. Hence both are necessary for the progress of country."
2. *Report on the Post-War Educational Development in India* (1944): The report is popularly known as Sargent Report after Sir John Sargent, the then Educational advisor to the Government of India.

DEMERITS/LIMITATIONS/NEGATIVE EFFECTS OF THE SYSTEM OF EDUCATION DURING THE BRITISH PERIOD

According to H.H. Howell, "Education in India under the British Government was first ignored, then violently and successfully opposed and conducted on system now universally admitted to be erroneous". ('*Education in British India, 1872*')

Gandhiji in '*Basic Education*' observed, "The foundation that Macaulay laid of education has enslaved us." He further said, I am convinced that the present system of education is not only wasteful but positively harmful. Most of the boys are lost to the parents and to the occupations to which they were born. They pick up evil habits, effect urban ways and get a smattering something which may be anything but education." Gandhiji again writes, "The present system of education does not meet the requirements of the country in any shape or form. English has been medium of education in all the highest branches of learning, has created a permanent bar between the highly educated few and the uneducated many." He further ads, "We have up to now concentrated stuffing children's minds with all kinds of information without even thinking or stimulating or developing them. Let us now cry a halt and concentrate on educating the child properly through manual work not as a side activity but as a prime means of intellectual activity."

Nurullah and Naik found the following defects:

1. It failed to evolve a national system of education;
2. It failed to realise the place of India in the comity of nations;
3. It failed to evolve a synthesis of East and West;
4. It had inadequate aims;
5. It adopted the downward filtration theory which gave a set back to mass education;

6. It failed to develop India socially, economically or politically;
7. It failed to evolve any plan of educational development. "Policies came and went with successive Governor-Generals or Directors of Public Instruction. The Kaleidoscopic background made long-range planning impossible and had disastrous consequences on the progress of Indian education".

Prof. Aparna Basu of Delhi University in her publication '*Essays on the History of Indian Education*' (1982) has observed. "Negative effects are fairly obvious. The educational system by building up an educated elite and neglecting popular education helped to preserve and strengthen the barrier between the upper classes and the masses. The use of English raised the class barrier even higher. The low rate of literacy, the method of teaching, neglect of training of teachers, contempt for manual work, emphasis on a literary education and neglect of technical education which was inevitable in a colonial context, and the creation of a gulf between an elite educated in English and the masses—all these constituted formidable obstacles in the path of development."

Following defects are usually pointed out:

1. There was no system of national education. It was an un-Indian system of education.
2. It was an urban system of education in a rural country.
3. The curriculum was English dominated.
4. The system was too literary and bookish.
5. The system neglected citizenship training.
6. The system was very wasteful.
7. The system followed a single track.
8. The system was unplanned.
9. The system was very expensive.

10. The system was not in accordance with the needs of a secular democratic country.
11. It emphasised rote memory.
12. It neglected technical and vocational education.
13. Its reach was very unlimited. Majority of the population remained illiterate.
14. It neglected the study of cultural heritage of India.
15. It created barriers between the few educated and the illiterate many.

A graphic image of English education initiated Indian of the early 20th century is given by Anand K. Coomarswamy in 1908. He writes:

"Speak to the ordinary graduate of an Indian University, or a student from Ceylon, of the ideals of the Mahabharata – he will hasten to display his knowledge of Shakespeare: talk to him of religious philosophy – you find that he is an atheist of the crude type common in Europe a generation ago, and that not only has he no religion, but is lacking in philosophy as the average Englishman : talk to him of Indian music – he will produce a gramophone or a harmonium, and inflict upon you one or both; talk to him of Indian dress or jewellery – he will tell you that they are uncivilised and barbaric; talk to him of Indian art – it is news to him that such a thing exists; ask him to translate for you a letter written in his own mother tongue – he does not know it. He is indeed a stranger in his own land." ('*Modern Review*', Calcutta, Vol. 4, Oct. 1908, p. 338)

While delivering a series of lectures in 1912, practically after a century of the event of manipulating and introducing English system of Education in India, J.N. Farquhar wrote:

"The new educational policy of the Government created during these years the modern educated class of India. These are men who think and speak in English habitually, who are proud of their citizenship in the British Empire, who are devoted to English literature, and whose intellectual life has been almost entirely formed by the thought of the West, large numbers of them enter government services, while the rest practise law, medicine or teaching, or take to journalism or business. We must also note that the powerful excitement which has sufficed to create the religious movements we have to deal with is almost entirely confined to those who had an English education," (J.N. Farquhar,) "*Modern Religious Movements in India*" first published in England in 1914, first Indian Edition.

Munshiram Manoharlal, Delhi, 1967, quoted by Jeevan Kulkarni in '*Historical Truths and Untruths Exposed*', 1991: "It failed to develop India economically

MERITS OF THE SYSTEM OF EDUCATION

Prof. Aparna Basu described the merits as, "The introduction of English education as one of the series of acts positively opened the doors of the West to the East. In every sphere of modern Indian life, though the influence of tradition persists, the impact of the west can also be traced. Much of the organization of the democratic state, its secular character, the structure of its institutions and the political principles underlying them are all largely European in inspiration. Similarly, the social reforms in Hindu society, the movements for the emancipation of women and for the removal of untouchability reflect western influence to a considerable extent."

The merits of the system of education may be summarised as:

1. The system promoted Western knowledge and science among the Indians, which broadened their outlook in life.
2. English education brought about a re-awakening and a desire among the people of India to recaputure their past glory.

3. Contact with Western thought helped to develop democratic and liberal ideas among the Indians.
4. English education re-kindled in the people the spirit of nationalism. By and large, national movement was led by leaders who had received their education through the English medium and were well-versed with Western political thoughts.
5. A uniform system of education through English medium educational institutions brought the people of different provinces together and they waged the freedom struggle.
6. According to Nurullah and Naik, "It freed the Indian mind from the "thraldom of old fashioned ideas" and laid the foundations of a Renaissance in modern Indian life."

Expansion of Educational Facilities (1855-56 to 1946-47)

Table 8.1: Educational Institution (1855-56 to 1946-47)

		1855-56	*1901-02*	*1921-22*	*1946-47*
1.	Universities	—	5	14	17
2.	Colleges of General Education	21	145	172	496
3.	Colleges of Professional and Other Education	13	46	74	130
4.	Secondary Schools (General)	281	1,170	1,248	5,297
5.	Secondary Schools (Vocational and Technical)	—	94	292	665
6.	Special and other Schools	7	990	3,729	4,746
7.	Middle Schools	—	4,323	6,739	11,162
8.	Primary Schools	50,676	97,854	160,070	172,681

Table 8.2: Expansion of Primary Education (1937-47)

Year	*No. of Primary Schools*	*No. of Pupils*
1881-82	82,916	2,061,541
1901-02	97,854	3,204,336
1921-22	1,60,070	6,310,400
1936-37	1,97,227	10,541,790
1946-47	1,72, 681	13,036,248

Source: 'Second Yearbook: Elementary Education' (1964), NCERT, New Delhi.

Table 8.3: Enrolment by Stages (1855-56 to 1946-47)

	1855-56	1901-02	1921-22	1946-47
1. University				
(i) Total	4,355	23,007	57,837	237,546
(ii) Girls	N.A.	264	1,529	23,207
2. Secondary Stage:				
(i) Total	33,801	82,312	218,606	370,812
(ii) Girls	N.A.	1,677	5,818	83,270
3. Middle School Stage:				
(i) Total	—	1,080,670	385,372	2,036,109
(ii) Girls	—	8,133	24,655	281,606
4. Primary School Stage:				
(i) Total	885,624	3,564,122	6,404,200	14,105,418
(ii) Girls	—	380,282	1,297,643	3,728,793

Note: Enrolment of pupils at the primary stage includes enrolment in primary departments of secondary stage.

Sourcess:

(1) Basu, Aparna, '*Essays in the History of Indian Education*' 1981.

(2) Nurullah and Naik in '*A Students' History of Education in India*' 1949 gives the number of Universities as 19 with 241,794 students.

(3) '*The Education Commission 1964-66*' puts the number of Universities at 20.

Dr. Veena Bhalla of the Association of Indian Universities, New Delhi, gives the following figures for the year 1947 in '*University News*', 39(2), January 08, 2001.

(i)	Students enrolled in General Higher Education	183238
(ii)	Students enrolled in professional/Special Higher Education	45643
	Total	228881

Table 8.3: Sexwise Middle and High Schools 1946-47

Type of Schools	Number			Enrolment		
	Boys	Girls	Total	Boys	Girls	Total
Middle English Schools	4,169	620	4,789	5,40,441	85,484	6,25,925
Middle Vernacular Schools	2,914	567	3,481	4,04,377	92,300	4,96,677
High Schools	3,061	576	3,637	13,81,038	1,78,341	15,59,279
Total for 1946-47	10,144	1,763	11,907	23,25,836	3,56,125	26,81,981
Total for 1936-37		13,036				22,87,872

Source: Nurullah and Naik (United Punjab).

It is difficult to compare the statistics of 1946-47 with those of 1936-37 on account of the creation of Pakistan.

General Observations on the Expansion of Educational Facilities

1. It was slow between 1813 and 1854 on account of controversies over goals, methods, contents and organisation of education.
2. Real growth started with the creation of Education Departments in 1855.
3. Establishment of universities at Calcutta, Bombay and Madras in 1857 promoted higher education.
4. From 1921 to 1947, privately managed schools and colleges with or without government aid played an active role in the expansion of education.
5. Higher education was widely diffused in Bengal.
6. Education had a predominantly literary bias.
7. Primary education was not wide-spread.
8. Agricultural education received little attention.
9. Technological subjects were by and large excluded from the curriculum.
10. Concentration on urbanised upper and middle classes led to the neglect of mass education.
11. Literacy rate remained very low.

In 1931, the percentage of literacy was 7% and in 1941 it rose to 12.2 percent.

It is difficult to compare the statistics of 1946-47 with those of 1936-37 on account of the creation of Pakistan.

General Observations on the Expansion of Educational Facilities

1. It was slow between 1813 and 1854 on account of controversies over goals, methods, contents and organisation of education.
2. Real growth started with the creation of Education Departments in 1855.
3. Establishment of universities at Calcutta, Bombay and Madras in 1857 promoted higher education.
4. From 1921 to 1947, privately managed schools and colleges with or without government aid played an active role in the expansion of education.
5. Higher education was widely diffused in Bengal.
6. Education had a predominantly literary bias.
7. Primary education was not wide-spread.
8. Agricultural education received little attention.
9. Technological subjects were by and large excluded from the curriculum.
10. Concentration on urbanised upper and middle classes led to the neglect of mass education.
11. Literacy rate remained very low.

In 1921, the percentage of literacy was [illegible] and in 1941 it rose to 12.2 percent.